*The Valley Loses
Its Atmosphere*

Winétt de Rokha

El valle pierde su atmósfera

1943–1946

Winétt de Rokha

The Valley Loses Its Atmosphere

1943–1946

translated from Spanish by
Jessica Sequeira

Shearsman Books

First published in the United Kingdom in 2021 by
Shearsman Books Ltd
PO Box 4239
Swindon
SN3 9FN

Shearsman Books Ltd Registered Office
30–31 St. James Place, Mangotsfield, Bristol BS16 9JB
(this address not for correspondence)

www.shearsman.com

ISBN 978-1-84861-783-4

Original poems copyright © Herederos de Winétt de Rokha.
Todos derechos reservados. All rights reserved.

Translation and Introduction copyright © Jessica Sequeira, 2021

The right of Jessica Sequeira to be identified as the translator of this work, and as the author of the introduction, has been asserted by her in accordance with the Copyrights, Designs and Patents Act of 1988.
All rights reserved.

El valle pierde su atmósfera was first published as part of *Arenga sobre el arte*
by the author's husband, Pablo de Rokha (Santiago: Multitud, 1949), and was reprinted in Winétt de Rokha's posthumous Collected Poems, *Suma y destino* (Santiago, Multitud, 1951).

We are grateful to the Fundación de Rokha, and its director,
Patricia Tagle de Rokha, for granting us permission to publish this
translation of Winétt de Rokha's work.

Winétt de Rokha and Her Canto Americano

The Valley Loses Its Atmosphere by the Chilean poet Winétt de Rokha (1894–1951) is a book of 48 poems written primarily during her journey across Latin America. Winétt's husband Pablo had been named Cultural Ambassador of Chile in the Americas by President Juan Antonio Ríos, and together the couple visited nineteen countries, getting to know cities and villages, meeting people, giving talks, attending dinners, and writing lots of poetry as they went along. According to the Chilean writer Álvaro Bisama: "The trip, previously unthinkable, takes place thanks to the effect of [a translated anthology called] *12 Spanish American Poets* on the Chilean cultural scene, which was impressed by De Rokha's inclusion. Mario Ferrero says that as a result, President Juan Antonio Ríos called to the poet and proposed 'a secret mission of a cultural nature, to be developed across the different countries of América'." De Rokha accepted this mission, and his travels with Winétt, from 1944 to 1946, took them through South America and Central America – including Peru, Uruguay, Bolivia, Colombia, Venezuela, Ecuador, Guatemala, Cuba and Mexico – before reaching the U.S.A. On 27 November 1945 the couple read their poetry at the Library of Congress in the United States, and a recording exists of this moment in which one marvels at their remarkably similar rhythms and cadences. For an anecdotal and picaresque account of the couple's time in these places, I recommend Pablo de Rokha's autobiography *El amigo piedra*.

Begun just before the journey, Winétt de Rokha's *The Valley Loses Its Atmosphere* contains the full richness of her impressions transformed into language, with an abundant layering of phrase upon phrase to create a lush and hypnotic effect. Winétt's introductory poem announces the intention to create a "song of gold dust" and a "strophe of the day's necessity". "*The Valley Loses Its Atmosphere* is incorruptibly American," she proclaims. The poems make reference to different parts of "América", with an attention to the land and social conditions, mentioning the "banana plantations, rubber plantations, farmlands that produce bloodsuckers", the indigenous peoples such as the *jivaro* of Peru and Ecuador, local fauna like wolves and wasps, local flora like the *clavel del aire* or *copihue*, and popular protests like the Baltimore Workers' Congress. Given the context, the special attention afforded to communism is unsurprising, from the naming of leaders like Lenin and Stalin to the evocation of inequalities that need to be changed. There are also digs at bourgeois women writers such as Angélica Arenal. At one level, this is the wondrous *costumbrismo* of a woman actively recording what she sees as she makes her way across territories new to her. But the deliberate density of references and heaping up of phrases makes this far more than just a log, to the point that signifier is often hard to connect signified – this book of poems is engaged in a different kind of labour.

For me, it's astonishing that Winétt de Rokha's work has not been taken seriously until now as a *canto americano,* an epic poem that sings of a united América through its land and peoples, replicating through its prose the very processes of contradiction and transformation that have been undergone by history itself. The *canto americano* is a fascinating form taken up in different ways by figures during this period, in the attempt to craft a fluid identity for an América which tended to be defined through ties of brother- and sisterhood and connections with nature, against what we might now call the extractivist practices of foreign corporations, particularly the United States. Such ties tend to seek forms of belonging and togetherness that go beyond both capitalism and nationhood, even if the individual authors feel loyalty to specific regions in both their physical landscape and evoked imaginaries. Winétt de Rokha's *The Valley Loses Its Atmosphere* (1949) takes up different places in their lived detail, and is not interested in the major monuments of the tourist guides but in incredibly specific and surprising details, whose quasi-surreality is amplified by the way she describes them; it puts her in a tradition with Pablo Neruda (*Canto General,* 1950) and Gabriela Mistral (*Poema de Chile,* 1967), among others. Neruda speaks in passionate monologues and dedications to friends and historical figures about a land that contains the dead and history but is forever capable of resurrection, while Mistral speaks in a tender conversation between a ghost, an indigenous boy and a deer. But there is a shared interested in linking geographic, social and psychological landscapes, and their project of creating a *canto americano* is also the project of creating an América.

It is notable that the de Rokha couple, husband and wife, adopted the *canto americano* before Neruda and Mistral, and developed their works near simultaneously. Their writing is so united it is almost impossible to speak about them separately, as they influenced one another, travelling and living together, with a significant overlap in both political and domestic material. They also share many stylistic similarities, including the lengthy line bordering on prose and the preference for specific words like "symphony". Yet taking the two together has tended to obscure the perhaps more interesting differences. Pablo de Rokha's works most explicitly about América (*Canto al Ejército Rojo,* 1944; *Los poemas continentales,* 1944–1945; *Interpretación dialéctica de América y los cinco estilos del Pacífico,* 1947; *Carta Magna del continente,* 1949; *Arenga sobre el arte,* 1949; and the prose work *El amigo piedra*) speak in a tragic, rage-filled, frequently aggressive howl of denouncement, punctuated by phrases of incredibly lyrical beauty and ethical content; he frequently takes on the position of a wounded bull, capricious and unpredictable, but full of moral convictions.

Winétt speaks in measured, lyrical, melancholy tones, but her patient and sensual formulations are no less intense. Although her register often remains cryptic, without elucidation or epiphany, her writing seems not so much one of denouncement as of creation, proposing a new kind of language and a new kind of person, within new economic structures. And the way that Winétt's work creates this new form of agency is through her performance of neobaroque rhetoric. The Latin American neobaroque is often associated, and is theoretically worked by the Cuban writer José Lezama Lima, who linked it in philosophical essays, particularly in his masterpiece *La expresión americana*, to a potential that was at once liberatory, revolutionary and spiritual. Winétt's work precedes and shares affinities with Lezama Lima's ideas of a "gnostic space" and incarnates a new world through the creation of language, as well as with common with the baroque lyricism and historical atmospheres of Alejo Carpentier.

This is a world in which the human wanders through the landscape as a nomad, specifically the geographies of Latin America, gathering them up, formulating them in language, and returning them to the world as she continues to move. Chaos and clarity, dissonance and harmony, meaning and non-meaning are in a relationship here, with their eroticisms and complications. This is not recollection in tranquility; rather, the baroque stylings and patterns resist what is static, with a hungry capacity to include and speak of everything it comes across, not necessarily giving it the artificial order of the encyclopaedia or natural history tract, but marvelling at all that can exist or be imagined. Winétt and Pablo, outside of their country of origin, Chile, experience the internationalism of the Communist Party not as utopia but as lived experience, the vivid fullness of time recounted. Their language is anything but the bureaucratic legalese of the nation-state or Politburo, and seems to reject all too rigid allegiances. Indeed, in *El amigo piedra* Pablo de Rokha notes their detachment from Chile as they left, looking down from the airplane window: "The flag of Chile is a handkerchief the size of the world as we reach the border, cross over it and do not cry".

What is the América that Winétt finds? There is a mottled variety to it, "jumbled qualities". It is a "convulsive labyrinth, uneven, baroque, communicating". The multiplicity of América resists order, yet is not quite chaos. One feels her pleasure in making her way across an América whose territories had already been given a hundred names by indigenous peoples before Columbus arrived, and have taken on thousands since, as she makes visits on behalf of a Party that in theory stands for the friendship of peoples and the pursuit of economic and social justice. Winétt and Pablo both write positively of Stalin and his project of collectivisation, the darker aspects of which had not fully come to public light at that time; when they travelled, the Gulags were operating in full force, processing millions of people, but these facts were not yet acknowledged by the Communist Party or by the majority of intellectuals. Now this might change our subsequent reading of the text, which make Winétt's mentions in this regard seem innocent or naïve, but they are part of the grain of the time.

Winétt's focus, however, remains on América, in which wonders and disparities alike were in plain view. The question is how to write about them during such a whirlwind tour, doing justice to what she saw but at the same time molding them into something different. Winétt's repeated discoveries of mental images in writing are nothing like what a conquistador's discovery would have been. Her discoveries as a traveller take place, in contrast, in a poetic nonlinear time, in which there isn't a pioneer mentality of singular discovery, but constant revelation. She and Pablo travel without the desire to dominate, without everything parceled out and separated as text. The notion of text itself can be used for many purposes. Parchments and manuscripts appear throughout *The Valley Loses Its Atmosphere*, linked to legal histories and colonial and constitutional realities, but Winétt's own book presents another kind of manuscript, with its voices of jobless people and animals and geographies, "voices resurrected from a past hammered into rustic prose".

And this prose style itself, this cobbling and hammering and heaping up, is *doing* something. It is a "lineage of the popular avant-garde", as Winétt puts it, one that is lovingly glued together from the abundance of found elements and nature, "dark vegetations of awe". The prose itself becomes a force that bursts out of the static perfection of the blank page, and out of the expectations of the perfectly crafted verse of her period, to make things happen. Its excess resists the gelling and consolidation of experience at multiple levels, to create a shifting and liquid fluidity open to change. The imagery of a phrase itself is unexpected, and this unexpectedness is then juxtaposed in surprising ways with other startling images. In this not-totally comprehensible, not-totally mapped out reality, the reader feels slightly bewildered. Yet for one who is not a cartographer or explorer, who is not looking for a guidebook or tourist manual, this can be an exciting feeling. You can arrive at not just new places but also a new idea of time, with a feeling of comprehension ever on the brink: "destiny without resolve", "insurgent sepias", or "the firewood of what's past and the emblem of defined uncertainty" as Winétt puts it, a piling up of stiff technique to set it alight.

Here is where Winétt's idea of a non-individualist subject with a different agency comes in, one that is porous and entwined with the elements of reality, the opposite of a single identity and "I". She repeatedly criticises the idea of the "hero", the "suffering woman", the atom, the "allegorical membranous mob", the "disjointed, Jesuit" approach to thinking, and anything else that favors abstraction and singularity over concrete and interconnected projects. The form of subjectivity she presents, what she calls an "open self", remains uncertain and fluid, not fixed within its own boundaries but connected to the places, animals, plants and other people around it. Notably, Winétt mentions "Whitman, de Rokha, Mayakovsky, the whole social foliage flowering, bearing fruit". Awareness of a historical situation forms a large role in producing artistic and literary creation, and while it is true that certain poets have made poems that are especially beautiful or that achieve special success, both "beauty" and "success" inevitably exist within their circumstances. The same critique of the Great Poet can be made of the Great Revolution. It is the build-up of context that produces an event; it does not make sense to only romanticise the writer or event in itself.

So how to think about change? This is a delicate matter, requiring an attention to concrete individual things, but not at the expense of their interweaving with the rest. Winétt's interest is in the relational, the way that the single and the many are related. Each phrase of hers is unique and surprising, but each of these phrases also forms part of a much larger network of other phrases. All the little things matter, everything forms part of an evolving system. And Winétt's phrases, individually light yet building into a powerful density, are a patient yet insistent remaking of both Latin America and Winétt as a subject, in concrete relation to what is around her.

Here Winétt's style embodies a deep philosophy that questions the validity of the reified and fully formed idea, including the idea of self. Contradiction and jumble are required for movement. Clots of impressions push actions into being. No small thing is negligible, and the sum of all the stuff and thoughts together creates a force larger than each thing. Something uniform and clearly defined as a single identity does not move. It is accumulation, a departure from the approach of progressive narrative and linear time, a "heaped-up transcendental insistence" that mobilises the unstoppable, powerful, oceanic force that can sweep away old ideas and sweep in new ones. This style of a dialectic in movement is coherent with Winétt's communist and revolutionary beliefs, but they also express her own sensibility, in which the intuition she mentions in her introductory poem combines with a certain will in order to create – not on one's own but, inseparably, in conversation with others.

And the rhetoric of movement maps onto an idea of growth. América is described as "luscious fruits on the path to becoming fruits", and there is a poem dedicated to Pablo that mentions the "childhood" of América. "América" refers primarily to Latin America, yet given that Winétt and Pablo reached the United States, met comrades and gave a reading there, perhaps they also entertained a unified vision of South, Central and North despite their suspicions of that region's economic practices. The world, shaken by recent and ongoing civil and world wars as Winétt and Pablo travelled, seemed to vibrate with imminent catastrophe and change. Pablo's notes on their time in this América reflect this, as for instance when he speaks of Winétt's and his talk at the Universidad Interamericana: "We are giving a talk here, shaking from the heat and pain of the vast south, in a town where everything in the world is confusion."

These ideas of systemic and evolutionary change also, perhaps, inform Winétt's relationship with Pablo, a "melodic marriage that contradicts itself, in belief, a system". She also writes: "To be pregnant, have something develop, the sensuality of ideas bearing fruit". Winétt knew something about this, as she had nine children by Pablo. Indeed, in many ways the categories of personal relationships and the development of América map onto one another in Winétt's work as forms of love and development. Winétt co-ran the magazine and publishing project *Multitud* with Pablo for many years, and herself contributed to it. Born to a slightly higher social class than him, she resisted the role of a bourgeois wife and threw herself into a life of immense creativity, including opinionated arguments and critiques. Things were not always easy. Pablo de Rokha inhabited the world of the *huaso*, a Chilean type associated with the provincial and with living close to the earth, as opposed to the elegant, dandyish, European-admiring bohemians of Santiago of which he counted Neruda as one, a notion behind some of his most untrammelled attacks. Winétt and Pablo shared a poor but happy family life in the countryside, with Pablo travelling to sell books and used artworks and Winétt raising the large family. (Sometimes she also accompanied him.) Bisama recounts one period when they had to survive on tremendous and ultimately nauseating quantities of avocados. Pablo printed his own writings and sold those of others. He did the same for paintings, falsifying quite a few canvases and claiming they were works by well-known artists. The premature deaths of some of their children, as well as Pablo's fickleness, sent her into moods of depression and oneiric writing, as one sees most clearly in her book *Oniromancia*. Yet the stereotype of Winétt, that she was only a melancholy, dutiful wife and mother, is belied by these vigorous verses and her calls for social change. And she too could be quite scathing, as when, at one point in their journey across Latin America, she was summoned to the embassy to be reprimanded for accusing other women of being bourgeois, a form of attack she had also made previously in the pages of *Multitud* and which appears in veiled form in this book.

Although Winétt was not primarily concerned with her own autobiography, her work does contain references to her life and experiences. In *The Valley Loses Its Atmosphere* she ironically describes herself as a "fearful vestal virgin" surrounded by "martial illusions", with "fingernails of Scottish origin", and as an "absurd woman with provincial anguish". Her emphasis on, and affiliation with, the province is notable; in *The Valley Loses Its Atmosphere* it is defended against the city, depicted as full of pomp. The village is lethargic and slow, yet once it moves, it does so completely. The huge rolling build-up of the storm leads to a spasm; the "languor" becomes a "spilling-over". The force of the "provincial steed" (Pablo or communism, perhaps) will charge against the "urban shell" and "the worn-out language of hunched cetaceans with fancy dress and culture". City life, in contrast, shelters the "conceited Narcissus of intellectual foliage" who changes his accent, and the "dead literary gathering" of poets seeking only their own glory. Similarly Winétt pokes fun at the ancestral, archaic bugler who loves pink corseted women, and at other outdated figures who merely replicate rather than creating something new, individualists "lacking universal subjects". Winétt's critique isn't of the pretentiousness of these figures (and after all, isn't pretentiousness ambition? isn't pretentiousness a striving towards a reality that doesn't yet exist? isn't pretentiousness to be celebrated?) but just the opposite, a lament for their complacence and lack of desire to stretch towards anything outside of their zone of comfort. For similar reasons she was also critical of books like Jorge Isaac's popular novel *María*, a classic of Latin American romanticism.

A book-length critical study by Javier Bello, which shares the name of this book, gathers Winétt's works into one place with a short biographical introduction as well as a few critical studies by scholars. This is the most serious book published on the poet's work to date. Bello argues that: "The reception of Winétt de Rokha's work over the past 55 years has been almost non-existent… Winétt was never truly read, beyond her external attributes." He refers to the very superficial texts by Winétt's contemporaries Manuel

Magallanes Moure and Juan de Luigi, who seem more concerned with Winétt's looks, and her qualities as a muse, than her books. These ideas still exist in insidious ways; talking to a few Chilean poet friends about this translation just a few months ago, they opined that if Pablo de Rokha is red wine, Winétt de Rokha is a rosé. In my view, the rigour and originality of her writing have been insufficiently recognised.

Bello takes a crack at a more generous reading, saying that: "*The Valley Loses Its Atmosphere* is a book that will require many readings to give an account of its complexity and restore it to the place I believe it should have held – and should still hold – in contemporary Chilean poetry, as one of its most intense and particular moments." His introductory essay moves in this direction but ultimately is more concerned with recuperating Winétt as a poetic figure in general, taking a more biographical approach that doesn't go too deeply into the work itself. This also holds for the other secondary readings contained in the book, by Soledad Falabella, Juan G. Gelpí, Ángeles Mateo del Pino, Jorge Monteleone, Eliana Orgega and Adriana Valdés, which make strong arguments for the value of Winétt's work but do not really give the book a close reading or analyze its formal elements. Winétt de Rokha is read as a figure in the context of a larger discussion about women and Latin America – not problematic in itself, but if a writer is going to be recuperated, her work needs to be read closely as well. Much work remains to be done in this sense, given that Winétt and many other women writers are still relegated to being read as women first. Perhaps we can start with an attitude like Vicente Huidobro's, a reader who took Winétt's work seriously. In an interview with *La Nación* on 28 May 1939, Huidobro says that for him the *poetas verdaderos* (true poets) are Winétt de Rokha and Rosamel del Valle, and that their writing for him is *sin dulzainas gelatinosas ni barro verde* ("without jellied oboes or green mud"), a poetic hymn to poetry.

The question of how Winétt balanced her own form of rigour and originality – her own kind of red wine – with her interests in the baroque, in América, in history and in dream life as in her book *Oniromancia,* is ripe for much more commentary. Her husband's looming presence somewhat blocks the view. Precisely because Pablo's own writing is so defiant, not to mention prolific, his story has tended to craft our understanding of hers. His relationship with the Communist Party was complex, and he became a member under the regime of President Pedro Aguirre Cerda but was expelled due to his vocal criticisms of certain members, whom he saw as dinosaurs. The invitation to go on the Latin America trip was a welcoming back to the fold, in a way, one soon cast into doubt upon their return when President Gabriel González Videla took power and began to actively repress and persecute members of the Communist Party. (This is when Neruda, famously, had to go into hiding and cross the cordillera to safety in Argentina.) Pablo de Rokha's political and emotional moods, and his depression and aggressive tendencies, grew more volatile during this period, aggravated by Winétt's death of cancer a few years after their return. His 1953 work *Fuego negro* was a long elegy about her and their love and comradeship, and his great 643-page anthology compiling his life's work, published the next year, was dedicated to Winétt and included multiple black and white images of her in its first pages. When Pablo killed himself a few years afterwards, he did so with the Smith & Wesson .45 calibre pistol with pearl handle given to him by the artist David Siqueiros and General Lázaro Cardenas, when he and Winétt had travelled through Mexico together, and he did so while gazing at a big portrait of Winétt. This story, repeated and retold by younger generations of poets, reaffirms the stereotype of Winétt as Pablo's companion in tragedy. This may well be how Pablo thought of her, but modern readers are not limited to this interpretation.

 I bring up these matters of how to position Winétt's work because, left unaddressed, it would remain just as it has until now, negligible, unread, acknowledged as a peripheral curiosity. Latin American intellectual history itself has often been treated as peripheral to European intellectual history, with attention to projects such as the *canto americano* that grant a narrative to the land and peoples receiving new attention, in an attempt to change this. Yet the form itself also has been questioned, linked to the poet-prophet's voice speaking on behalf of the geography and oral traditions rather than letting them speak for themselves, and often leaving out women and indigenous peoples. At the same time, women's writing is often read a genre apart. To read Winétt de Rokha's *The Valley Loses Its Atmosphere* as a *canto americano* and an explicit contribution to literary and intellectual history opens it up to a new thickness of context, bringing it out of the gendered reading and off the pre-marked trails. Writing this translator's note has been an activity of exploration and discovery for me as much as the reader, a labour that could have been dispensed with – certainly, the book would have got out the door faster – but which I feel is necessary, especially for a writer like Winétt, for whom critical materials are spare and superficial. The reviewing culture is what it is, pressed for time and resources, but if you provide a framework the conversation can sometimes go further, not just sticking to what is said by the press release or dictated by idle habit. Winétt is not just worth recuperating as the talented wife of a talented famous poet, or as an important forgotten women writer. That argument is not enough; it ignores the text itself. Critical writing is about moving the conversation into richer, stranger, more specific, more complex terrains, and if a translator's note can even partially suggest unsuspected geographies or other possible avant-gardes, I am happy to have written it. May the prolongation of ideas and the potency of interpretation flourish.

Jessica Sequeira

Works Cited

Bisama, Álvaro. 2021. *Mala lengua. Un retrato de Pablo de Rokha*. Santiago de Chile: Alfaguara.
de Rokha, Pablo. 1954. *Antología 1916–1953*. Santiago de Chile: Editorial Multitud.
de Rokha, Pablo. 1949. *Arenga del arte* containing *El valle pierde su atmósfera*. Santiago de Chile: Editorial Multitud.
de Rokha, Pablo. 1952. *Fuego negro*. Santiago de Chile: Editorial Multitud.
de Rokha, Pablo. 1951. *Suma y destino*, prologue by Juan de Luigi. Santiago: Editorial Multitud.
de Rokha, Pablo. 1990. *El amigo piedra, autobiografía*, prologue by Naín Nómez. Santiago de Chile: Editorial Pehuén.
de Rokha, Winétt. 2008. *El valle pierde su atmósfera*. In *Winétt de Rokha: El valle pierde su atmósfera. Edición crítica de la obra poética*, edited by Javier Bello. Santiago de Chile: Editorial Cuarto Propio.
de Rokha, Winétt. 2019. *Oneiromancy*, translated by Jessica Sequeira. Ripon: Smokestack Books.
Huidobro, Vicente. 2012. *Vicente Huidobro a la intemperie. Entrevistas, 1915–1946*, edited by Cecilia García-Huidobro. 2012. Santiago de Chile: Ocho Libros (Fundación Vicente Huidobro).

I am indebted to the website of the Universidad de Chile for its footnotes, which I have translated here, with slight modifications. The footnotes that begin with italicised words are my own additions.

Chronology

1894
Winétt de Rokha (Luisa Victoria Anabalón Sanderson) is born on 7 July to Indalecio Anábalón Urzúa, a colonel in the Chilean army, and Luisa Sanderson Mardones, a prominent society lady.

1914
Winétt's first verses, dedicated to Saint Francis of Assisi, are published in the magazine Zig-Zag. After reading them, Pablo de Rokha, a poet from Licantén in the south of Chile, comes to Santiago in search of their author.

1915
At 21 years old, Winétt publishes her first two books: *Horas de sol* (Hours of Sun) and *Lo que me dijo el silencio* (What the Silence Told Me), both under the pseudonym Juana Inés de la Cruz.

1916
Winétt marries Pablo de Rokha and adopts his surname as part of her new artistic name.

1917
Winétt's poems are included in the anthology of poems *Selva lírica* (Lyric Forest).

1927
Winétt publishes the long poem *Formas del sueño* (Forms of Dream).

1936
Winétt publishes 'Lenin', dedicated to the Russian revolutionary. The same year she publishes *Cantoral*, with a drawing on the cover by Pedro Olmos.

1939
Winétt and Pablo de Rokha found the publishing project *Multitud*, which prints magazines and books on and off until 1963. Its motto is 'Por el pan, la paz y la libertad del mundo' ('For bread, peace and the freedom of the world').

1943
Winétt publishes *Oniromancia* (Oneiromancy) with a drawing on the cover by Lukó de Rokha and a prologue by Pablo de Rokha.

1944–46
Winétt and Pablo begin a cultural tour which takes them to 19 countries in the Americas.

1949
Winétt's collection *El valle pierde su atmósfera* (The Valley Loses Its Atmosphere) is published inside Pablo de Rokha's book *Arenga sobre el arte* (Tirade on Art).

1951
Winétt de Rokha dies of cancer on 7 August. The same year, an anthology of her work titled *Suma y destino* (Sum and Destiny) is published, which includes poems from *Cantoral*, *Oniromancia*, *El valle pierde su atmósfera* and the unpublished collection *Los sellos arcanos* (The Arcane Seals).

1953
Pablo de Rokha publishes a prose poem, *Fuego negro* (Black Fire), in Winétt's memory.

Todo un canto nacido de polvo de oro, hilvanando
ordenación de arco-iris en fusa marina ex-divina
en la síntesis de la niñez ubérrima y triste, de cristal con lluvia.

Pergaminos no escritos, sonetos y vicisitudes,
adolescencia por el sueño determinada y sub-real.

Aguja y candente esplendor por cobijas de Invierno.

Cuando el medio siglo inicia su nocturno
de roedor imperturbable por mis venas de intermitente música,
canto mi tonada regular de horqueta para levantar océanos.

Stalin, en el balcón de los mundos futuros,
el león familiar del presente
cruza el espacio cargado de fulgores.

Por lo cual, "El Valle Pierde su Atmósfera"
es incorruptiblemente americano.

Flora como fauna y pájaros-árboles, aguas-vientos-soles,
mitos-símbolos, hombres tan civilizados cuanto salvajes,
ruinas, rascacielos, mares e inútiles espumas,
todo fundido en una aurora impresionante
renovaron los últimos saldos de mi personalidad de ojos celestes que dan mirada en negro.

Sin antepasados, crudo como cuero de sol,
canté-lloré mi libro todo para Pablo, mi compañero,
diciéndole cómo, paralela a su enorme acometida,
intuí y compuse la estrofa de la necesidad de la jornada.

WINETT

*All of it a song of gold dust, threading the rainbow
into the order of a demisemiquaver, ex-divine, of the sea,
into the synthesis of an abundant sad childhood, glass bespattered by rain.*

*Unwritten parchments, sonnets and vicissitudes,
adolescence in a particular sub-real dream.*

Needle and white-hot splendour through blankets of Winter.

*Whenever the half-century strikes up its nocturne
of a persistent rodent in my veins of intermittent music,
I sing my steady pitchfork melody to raise oceans.*

*Stalin, on the balcony of future worlds,
the familiar lion of the present,
can move through space, laden with brilliance.*

*And so "The Valley Loses Its Atmosphere"
is incorruptibly American.*

*Flora like fauna and bird-trees, water-wind-suns,
myth-symbols, man as civilised as he is savage,
ruins, skyscrapers, seas and useless foams,
everything melted into an astonishing dawn
revitalised what was left of my personality
with its light blue eyes that observe in black.*

*Without ancestors, raw as leather in the sun,
I sang-cried my book, everything for Pablo, my companion,
to tell him how in parallel with his huge assault,
here I am to intuit and compose the strophe of the day's necessity.*

                    WINETT

*

Un esquivo lucero favorito lustraba y enfocaba su farol,
lloraba la niebla intacta en sandalia caminante en escala mayor,
me invadía una vaga muselina opalescente, húmeda,
apretándome las formas disminuidas por cansancio.

Un dedo cortado dividíame los pétalos-labios,
catálogos de palabras surgían inarmónicos, reclutas,
cometa repleto, escudero alucinado, solo, erudito lobo,
clamaba en sinfonía de fuerte espectáculo mendigo.

Castañuelas líricas del alba y sus bellotas perezosas
ungían el tumultuoso despertar de los pueblos acrecentados por abajo, ayudantes, líderes.
Nieves densas, sin tiempo, emplumadas, envolturas claras que formulan
desde el rosa fingido, ululante, plañidero, de enjambre,
al cromo anaranjado depositario del abismo y la espuela.
Más tarde su lunar cronológico se tornó gris.

*

A favourite elusive star polished and focused its light
and an unbroken fog cried, wandering sandals on a major scale.
It filled me with a vague opalescent muslin, damp,
as it pressed shapes against me that slumped with fatigue.

When a cut finger divided my petal-lips,
catalogues of words streamed forth, atonal, summoned.
Brimming comet, delusional squire, lonely and erudite wolf,
I clamoured in the symphony of a loud beggar's performance.

Lyrical castanets of dawn and their idle acorns
anointed the tumultuous awakening of the peoples
who swelled from below, helpers, leaders.
Dense, timeless, feather-strewn snows, white sheath that forms
from the false and mournful shrieking of the pink hive
to become orange chrome, trove of abyss and spur.
In time its chronological beauty mark went grey.

*

Cielos, oleografías, escaramuzas, alaridos de corcho, teatro diáfano,
cofre de girasoles entrelazados, tejedor actual, parapeto,
rotundo pomo de alabastro pastoril, antología, técnica,
trébol pardo y ardiente en la concavidad dispersa de la pampa.
El desierto huidizo de botas que huyen, busca solución derivando en pañales
hacia las constelaciones del Pacífico en sermones de cartel,
monótono, monopolio, concierto de lejanías de sol tahúr
al paso de armas nómades en carrera alborotada de alhelíes.
Es el verde grande entre bastidores de yodo.
Inmensas contiendas en suspenso, Antofagasta[1], sonrisa de corsarios,
moho marítimo de minúsculas bahías sugerentes, universales,
con pasado de velas y ancianidad de jaguar paisano.
Un muñón industrial de trabajadores pulsa la cítara de sus pobladas pestañas humanas,
al encontrar recíproco el sistema de una nota alta, sepultada,
de cara sobre las rocas de mi niñez de estirpe de cuartel,
bóveda sin clérigos y el recuerdo frecuente de un muelle sumergido.

*

Heavens, oleographs, skirmishes, howls of cork, diaphanous theatre,
coffer of interlaced sunflowers, weaver of the moment, parapet,
round knob of pastoral alabaster, anthology, technique,
burning grey-brown clover in the pampa's scattered hollow.
The elusive desert of fleeing boots seeks a solution that ends in nappies,
towards the Pacific's constellations in signboard homilies,
monotonous, monopoly, the concert of distances of a gambler sun
at the pace of nomadic arms in a noisy race of wallflowers.
It's the vast green between frames of iodine.
Immense disputes in suspense, Antofagasta, smile of corsairs,
maritime mildew of tiny suggestive universal bays,
with a past of sails and the old age of a jaguar from your land.
An industrial trunnion of workers plucks at its zither of thick human eyelashes,
upon finding the reciprocal system of a high, concealed note,
face against the rocks of my childhood with a lineage of barracks,
crypt without priests and the frequent memory of a submerged dock.

*

Arica y su castaño tricolor se aureola en llamas y lanceta.
Muro y reloj de lo vivido forjado en pretérito con higos enterrado.

El boceto del árbol en exclamación piramidal de altar,
rompe la copla silvestre de lo estacionario y caduco por astucia,
abolengo de vanguardia popular.

El párpado cerrado sin modorra y carretera
ataca junto a su ancla, sin huella, en bancarrota de hiel,
enrostrando lo sedentario, generando con su estampa de ajedrez
un soplo de sopor abismal de la retina en derrotero, intervalo
sobre esas tierras sagradas, ásperas, de goma, de linterna,
soltando su girasol accidentado de o s c u r a s[1] vegetaciones de asombro.

Bienvenido, Lenin, bienvenido, tú, vencedor,
con tu puño y quijada segura, aboliendo miseria, argumento,
ya conduces y niquelas con tu radiación deslumbrante, de plan,
el vocablo flotante, enarbolado en disciplina, maniobra
donde me estrangulo, absurda de angustia provinciana.

*

Arica, tricolour brown, haloes itself in flames and a lancet.
The wall and clock of the living forged in the past with buried figs.

The sketch of a tree on the pyramidal exclamation of the altar
breaks the rustic song of what's stationary and antiquated, from cunning,
the lineage of the popular avant-garde.

The closed eyelid without drowsiness and route
attacks, joined to its anchor, without trace, in a bankruptcy of gall,
reproaching the sedentary, generating with its picture card of chess,
with the sigh of the enormous torpor of a retina on course, an interval
over those sacred, harsh lands of rubber, of lantern,
that release their troubled sunflower from dark vegetations of awe.

Welcome, Lenin, welcome, you, victor,
with your fist and sure jawbone, abolishing squalor, reason,
now you conduct and nickel-plate with your dazzling irradiance, with a plan,
the floating word, hoisted with discipline, a manoeuvre
in which I strangle myself, absurd woman with provincial anguish.

*

Anulo las cuerdas en el quitasol altisonante de la charla temprana
entre la música seria, de tambores y brindis federales, remos de Caronte,
de aquella y esta bárbara campana y su cuerno montañez.

Prisionera hojarasca de mi aspecto y su filo cerebral
cuando todos los sucesos-destinos en sacrificio de osamentas
se suicidan en el andamiaje forestal de los huesos…

Tanto "infierno blanco" tanto anuncio colérico, inofensivo,
agrietan, celosos, un motivo de humo, leche o cardo tibio.

Volcanes captan ardor en sorbos dramáticos, zarpazos
geológicamente de catástrofe, acumulando el huracán en vuelo,
dardo efímero, sellando un pacto con los cataclismos.
Ingenuamente me sonríe la "estrella solitaria" de índole republicana, sureña,
emparentada con vientos-pañuelos desplegados y lágrima.

*

I void strings in the high flown parasol of early chatter,
amidst serious music of drums and federal toasts, oars of Charon,
of that and this barbarous bell and its mountain horn.

Fallen-leaf prisoner to my appearance and its cerebral blade
when all events-fates in a sacrifice of skeleton
kill themselves, in the forest scaffolding of bones…

So much "white hell", so much furious, inoffensive announcement
crack open, jealous, a reason for smoke, milk or warm thistle.

Volcanoes capture ardour in dramatic gulps, blows,
geological catastrophe, the hurricane accumulating in flight,
ephemeral dart sealing a pact with the cataclysms.
Naïvely the "solitary star" of a republican, southern type smiles at me,
related to winds-kerchiefs, unfolded, a teardrop.

*

La marea y sus sables abrochan un relicario egregio, de logia,
en el mástil materialista, trizado de la tempestad y sus avispas feroces.
Lindo ciclamen, linda sonata, letanías amarillas, tajo del iris,
trapo, canela y perdón, hocico de foca virtuosa, orégano
con discursos estridentes, vaticinantes, roncos de mortaja,
van penetrando las vísceras de fósforo de museo con pellejo.
Dormito entre turbantes y pulseras calcáreas, sin rosario,
aun cuando la luz con su monarca decadente me complace realizándome.
El peñón incendiado del crepúsculo de esperma
se engaña vaporoso mientras la senda afligida, atisbando su alameda
arrastra su estopa ciega apagando candelabros fulgurantes
sobre canastos volcados en aceitunas de Otoño.

*

The tide and its sabres take hold of an eminent reliquary, from a lodge,
in the materialist mast, shattered by storm and its fierce wasps.
Pretty cyclamen, pretty sonata, yellow litanies, slash of iris,
rag, cinnamon and pardon, snout of virtuous seal, oregano
with strident, prophetic, hoarse discourses of shroud,
go penetrating the matchstick viscera of a museum with skin.
Dozing amidst turbans and limestone bracelets, without rosary,
even when light with its decadent monarch pleases me by fulfilling me.
The inflamed crag of the twilight of sperm
deceives itself, vaporous, as the sorrowful path, observing its boulevard,
hauls its blind tow, putting out shining candelabras
atop baskets spilling forth olives of Autumn.

*

Por los acantilados, orillando amapolas hostiles, resaca de ébano,
los paraguas de aquel castillo ensoberbecido, anónimo, rutilante, mortal de horcas cansadas.
Agonía de mañana, aspirando el retorno completo de las alondras cantábricas,
evocando el ósculo natal de tantas vírgenes incaicas, incensario,
relacionando tinieblas tenaces como moscas encapuchadas
que se llevaron el clamor sentimental de las pupilas
y la estatura vencida, en decadencia, por el tic-tac frondoso.
Un firmamento en júbilo, original, inmenso, de joyel,
pastoreaba las máquinas de acero ilustre y bayonetas
escoltando a Roosevelt, vecino paternal, unánime,
señalado ya por la caricia de entumecida postura
a cuestas de un ángel pregonero, perdido y enigmático.
Perfil marino, oxigenado, a mucha altura culpable,
bordando con filigranas de lógica las sienes triunfantes;
la salvia total, quemante, enfriada por meditación
en la bifurcación de petrificados oleajes antiguos.

*

By the cliffs, edging hostile poppies, ebony undertow, loom the parapets
of that arrogant, anonymous, glittering castle, fatal with worn-out gallows.
The morning's agony, breathing in the total return of Cantabria's larks,
evokes the native kiss of so many Incan virgins, an incense burner
that moves persistent shadows into relation, like the hooded flies
that stole away with the pupils' sentimental clamour,
and the stature defeated, through decadence, by the leafy tick-tock.
A rejoicing firmament, original, immense, with small jewels,
shepherded over the machines of illustrious steel and the bayonets
guarding Roosevelt, paternal neighbour, unanimous,
distinguished by his stiff postured caress
grasping the back of a heralding angel, lost and enigmatic.
Naval profile, oxygen-rich, guilty at a great height,
embroidering victorious temples with filigrees of logic;
the complete sage herb, scorching, chilled by meditation
in the bifurcations of ancient and petrified wave surges.

*

Maletas y calendarios victoriosos, pantallas míseras
confunden escaleras de nervios y vitrales de ámbar y verbena;
paredes de esponja con decoración en andrajos, invernaderos,
población de ventanas, en verdad, como ojos-brasas-hondos,
con suma ternura interior, de oreja, para refugio de fantasmas;
todo lo que eriza y abarca y define el apunte callado, serenata
del baúl de esmero de sus panoramas inmóviles.

Trepada por capítulo al mirador de las calandrias entre fusas y corcheas,
los pies curvos del planeta y su arco carpintero de kilómetros,
me sirven de pedestal, zapatos y punto de partida.

Veintitrés de noviembre con ración de pavo tradicional,
verduras amargas, nueces, castañas, mito, imbecilidad, cucharas,
pan prieto de festín, jalea, vino de tribu en copas delgadas,
bandeja de suspiros del May-flower y la piratería "bronté" del párroco.

*

Suitcases and victorious calendars, miserable screens
disorientate ladders of nerves and stained glass windows of amber and verbena;
walls of sponge with decor in rags, hothouses,
population of windows, to be honest, like eyes-coals-depths,
with supreme inner tenderness, of ear, for ghost refuge;
all that bristles and spans and defines the quiet outline, serenade
of the trunk with great care for its immobile scenes.

Scaled by chapter to the calandra larks' lookout, amidst demisemiquavers and quavers,
the planet's curved feet and its woodpecker arc of kilometres
serve me as pedestal, shoes and starting point.

Twenty-third of November with the serving of traditional turkey,
bitter greens, walnuts, chestnuts, myth, imbecility, spoons,
black bread to feast upon, jelly, tribal wine in slender glasses,
tray of sighs of the Mayflower and the "Brontë" piracy of the parish priest.

*

Lo santo con núcleo, imaginativo, "roto" laboratorio, poncho,
la alegría hermafrodita del petróleo lujurioso, harto, opaco,
y el azul-verde, ombligo protagonista de siete mares desertores.

¡Cuánta insistencia sumada, trascendental, documento maltratado
y alquimia acariciante posee mi afán de idolatría locuaz!

Terreno tétrico, esmirriado, seco, turbador, chacras,
canteras hirvientes, embalsamadas en abandono, nobles,
adoban un premio de siglos —mortaja de faraón— salitre, guano,
cuando la misma cauda entorpecedora, alerta, tubo-rancio,
pigmeo, exacto, todo lo iguala en caminata de ovejas.

El astro central arpegea en el piano marfileño, inquieto,
de la camanchaca incesante, palurdo ejemplo, rienda de atado
de un molino gigantesco girando su caballería del diablo
entre perlas profanas de academia.

Precipicio impulsivo, súplica para una muerte de epopeya y patíbulo espantoso.

*

Sacredness with a kernel, imaginative, "broken" laboratory, poncho,
hermaphroditic joy of lewd petroleum, fed up, opaque,
and the blue-green, protagonistic navel of seven deserting seas.

How much heaped-up transcendental insistence, abused document,
caressing alchemy there is in my zeal for loquacious devotion!

The dismal land, puny, arid, disturbing, of small farms
and boiling quarries, embalmed in neglect, noble,
prepares a prize of centuries – pharaoh's shroud – saltpetre, guano,
when the same sluggish yet alert dress train, stinking-pipe,
pygmy, exactly, in all things just like the rambling of sheep.

The central star plays arpeggios on the ivory-like piano, restless,
in incessant thick fog, typical hayseed, rein strapped
to a gigantic windmill spinning its devil's cavalry
amidst the academy's profane pearls.

Impulsive cliff, petition for the death of an epic and atrocious scaffold.

*

Equidistantes muñones de yerbas hundidas, maduras y confitura,
disco al revés tapizado, mantón de Manila, campo en papel celofán,
Talara:[1] una interrogación del mundo con yankees sin platea y cartero.

Arenales encuadernados en solidez, encaramados, caracolas, compás,
montículos de librería los inventan riachuelos principiantes
cuyas orillas pastoras, escondidas del ramaje esotérico
ciñen la cintura quisquillosa de las playas con jinete y galgos.

Todas las cosas del éter, superficiales, van a nivel y alojan
su revólver en un sitio de batalla, simetría y son de aparecidos,
directamente a mi instinto que se invierte en manuscrito de promesas.

Reflejo-caperuza, orla de mi traje de gala, hilachas,
aleteo, oratorio de adioses crispados, témpanos, libreta,
temblor de ciudadanía múltiple, bajeles, lomas, quilla,
sobre cerrado, lacrado en la Nada acontecido.

---

[1] Provincia noroccidental del Departamento de Piura. Una de las provincias con mayor producción petrolera del Perú.

*

Equidistant stumps of buried herbs, ripe and jam,
inverted upholstered disc, Manila shawl, field in cellophane,
Talara:[1] an interrogation of the world with yankees, without orchestra stalls or postman.

Quicksands bound in solidity, raised up, seashells, compass,
mounds of bookstore invented by novice streams
whose shepherding banks, hidden from esoteric branches,
cling to the fussy waists of beaches with rider and greyhounds.

All things of ether, superficial, go to the level and accommodate
their revolver on a battle site, symmetry and sound of ghosts,
straight to my instinct that stakes itself on a manuscript of promises.

Reflection-hood, trimming for my formal dress, rags,
wingbeat, oratorio of tense goodbyes, ice floes, notebook,
tremor of multiple citizenship, boats, hillocks, keel,
closed envelope, sealed inside the Nothingness that's happened.

---

[1] Northeastern province of Peru. One of the country's most productive petroleum areas.

Hendiduras tajantes, roedoras, trazo rebelde, saliva, escolta pedregosa
de un túnel tornasol de aguardientes de acíbar, imperceptibles,
pretendiendo en vano saciar el ansia ploma de un paradojal veneno.
La editorial interna de los magos del sismo agitando su soda
sin freno, desatando brumosos los lomos de sus yeguas sudorosas.

Calor que incendió la propaganda tropical, manjar de zumos,
bajas estancias que despedazan exuberancias rugientes
que despojan y construyen sus lagunas de prueba honda.

Designio pretérito-efímero, perfume, oasis, cartel ígneo, granero shakesperiano.

Esquina de las amanecidas con rocío y urracas, naciente
foco lustral a horcajadas de lo sucedido en ala plúmbea de rigor.

Diploma de tamboril-tambor-dolor, pergamino cervantino
glosan la historia de una esmeralda joven y vocinglera
desmayada, con dientes, en la arena musical de las preocupaciones sufrientes.

*

Sharp fissures, rats, defiant penstroke, saliva, rocky escort
for the litmus paper tunnel of the liquor of sorrow, imperceptible,
attempting in vain to satisfy the heavy yearning for contradictory poison.
The internal editor of the earthquake's magicians shaking their soda ash
nonstop, setting free the backs of their sweaty mares in the fog.

Heat that inflamed tropical propaganda, ambrosia of juices,
quiet countrysides now torn apart by roaring exuberances
that carve out and pile up their lagoons of deep evidence.

Fleeting-historical design, perfume, oasis, fiery notice, Shakespearean silo.

Corner of the just-risen with dew and magpies, emerging
spotlight gleaming astride the event, on leaden wing of rigour.

Diploma of little drum-drum-dolour, Cervantine parchment
gloss the history of a sonorous young Esmeralda
who collapsed, baring teeth, in the musical theatre of suffering angst.

*

Desde la cumbre nidos de larvas cesantes en trinchera rugosa
y hogueras escondidas me abrazan en polvareda de avestruces.
Arqueados lotos forman un capuchón de ruidos célibes
a trechos y huecos centelleantes en la urbe desierta de epitalamios.

Envuelto en compactas vestiduras —malla y drama—
acurrucado en un terraplén de dioses indiferentes, centinelas,
el Chimborazo y su buitre pelado en el infierno
por la velocidad de los armiños.

Zonas de engarce y dominio, trágicas creaciones, malecón,
¿ámbito subordinado, terrores formales, cubo experimental,
mangas gelatinosas, permiso taciturno, molienda fina?

Incorporadas actitudes para el cántico trovero de epitafio,
tan violento en travesura pagana, colonias, estelas, equipaje,
alboradas muertas, templadas, entelequia, colcha, estandarte,
sábana sin mácula cruzada de rastros de serpientes voraces.

*

From the peak, nests of jobless grubs in rough trenches
and secret bonfires embrace me with the clamour of ostriches.
Arching lotuses form a hood of celibate noises
through stretches and twinkling hollows in the desert city of epithalamia.

Swathed in dense clothes – mesh and melodrama –
curled up on an embankment of uncaring gods, sentinels,
the Chimborazo[2] and its vulture are flayed in hell
by the quickness of stoats.

Linked and dominated zones, tragic creations, jetty,
are they subordinate range, legal terrors, experimental cube,
jellied sleeves, aloof permission, fine milling?

Embodied attitudes for the troubadour's song, an epitaph,
so violent in pagan mischief, colonies, vapour trails, luggage,
mild and murdered dawns; a pipe dream, duvet, banner,
stainless sheet crossed by the tracks of greedy snakes.

---

[2] *Chimborazo:* an inactive volcano in the Andes, in Ecuador.

*

La lira de algún satélite desfigurado, espoleado, declamador,
rompe circunferencias que arden, rotas; techumbres dan alivio
con un cohete de ultratumba en tapias aldeanas, coloradas.

Con su contorno sucio, de librea, una ciudad creciente, fábricas
con amplitud de calles hermanas por argolla y futuro de llagas:
faenas, hipotenusa, basura, movimiento en combate de agonía y círculos.

Completa humareda sorteada, panales al descubierto, enseñoreándose serenos, dolidos,
sobre promontorios sentados, indefensos en el pórtico carcomido.

Cartelones-lunados. Por el Guayas, la bagatela, los peligros,
la intermitencia, los telegramas y el rubro de alcatraces malditos.

Algo gime cruel, agrandado, en la garganta dentada, sanguinolenta,
de algunos peces cuadrados, artesanos, en navío de signos actores
la voz bordada de la criatura fea se mata quintaesenciada,
medrosa y espectacular en su desarrollo barato y vacante.

*

The lyre of some satellite, deformed, spurred on, reciting,
smashes through circumferences that blaze, annihilated; roofs provide solace
with a rocket from the afterlife, in the reddish adobe walls of villages.

With their dirty silhouette, like a uniform, a growing city, factories
broad as streets meet as sisters in their shackles, their future of afflictions:
chores, hypotenuse, trash, movements in the battle of agony and circles.

A total smoke cloud dodged, nappies out in the open, taking serene possession, in pain,
sitting atop promontories, defenceless in the worm-eaten portico.

Spattered-signboards. By the Guayas,[3] the knick-knack, the dangers,
the flashing light, the telegrams and the overhead of fiendish sea birds.

Something moans with cruelty, swollen in the toothy bloodstained throat
of a few square-shaped artisanal fishes, actors in a boat of signs,
as the ornamental voice of the ugly creature dies, made quintessence,
frightened and spectacular in its cheap vacant growth.

---

[3] *Guayas:* A river in Ecuador

*

¡Cómo eres ese indómito cuento en tertulia finada, con peineta,
nadie te supo escribir en el cuenco de una olla quebrada y sus gallinas de intriga!
¡Cómo eres celda-escena, cómo alféizar inagotable de florero
para una pomposa y añeja ventura sin espera de herencia![1]

Fachada sin gárgolas ni máscaras, rémora de gloria y trovador establo,
fusil secular y limpio entre remolinos vastos de filiación alterna.

Trujillo de Venezuela
polvo de lo encrucijado vernáculo, plaga de orgullo por suplicio.

Soneto de anchos colibríes, cadenas, tizana, sota de bastos,
diminuto y sinuoso caminar de juncos y medusas, placenta,
susurro de violetas tardías en pubertad, órgano, monjas,
voces resucitadas de un pasado clavado en prosa serrana
como colmillo torvo en el tiempo inmutable y fabuloso.

*

How much of an untamed story you are, at a dead literary gathering with its fancy comb,
no one knew you wrote on the hollow of a broken pot with scheming chickens!
How much of a prison-cell scene you are, how much the untiring window display of a florist
for a bombastic, aging wealth with no hope of inheritance!

Façade without gargoyles or masks, obstacle to glory and stable for troubadours,
clean and ancient rifle amidst vast whirlwinds of shifting ancestry.

Trujillo of Venezuela,
dust on the vernacular crossroads, plague of vanity through torture.

Sonnet of wide hummingbirds, chains, fruit drink,[4] jack of knaves,
tiny bending movements of reeds and jellyfish, placenta,
rustle of violets late to puberty, organ, nuns,
voices resurrected from a past hammered into rustic prose
as by a fierce tusk of times immutable and fantastic.

---

[4] *tizana:* A Venezuelan drink made of sliced fruits in orange juice mixed with grenadine.

*

Por su impertérrita jerarquía ciudadana, de soldado, el clarinero
destiñe su atavío de mofa con charol usado
administrando la militancia interpretativa del paisaje antiguo.
Porque él flagela la lombriz que transita pasiva, gateando,
ama la hembra de blusa rosa-té y corsé febricitante, acordonado,
y con el arrastre de su capa envejecida sin asuntos universales,
impone el eco ancestral de su tonada parnasiana y arcaica.
Estremecidos y oscilantes bordean la llanura y su césped,
demonios burlescos los columpian, aturdidos, altaneros, inzambos,
es un bosquejo de yeso circunstancial, limado o acaso incongruente.

Inquietud de lo cabizbajo y abrumado del narrador,
caravana erguida entre habitantes aires dosificados en fila india.
Jamás destruidos por aislamiento y reverso de medalla,
meditativos están en la corteza del ombú que los engarza a una dinámica inspiradora
confrontada, en teoría natural, al aborigen conmemorativo.

Materia negra, progresiva, de augural sonrisa dolorosa,
entre vergeles, panteones, montañas, espinales, chubascos,
donaire que toma su enfermizo color de centeno esparcido
en las ínsulas aterradoras de Walt Disney.
Mas la obsesión del nido de aserrín improvisado
insultando la "vieja casita" de platino y sus búfalos de matadero.

¡Oh! manto con frutos de delicias en trance de ser ideas,
marginalmente, superáis todo antecedente y nexo gavilán
de esta tal solapa jabonosa, porfiada, en túnel de carretel,

*

By means of his impassive civic hierarchy, soldier-like, the bugler
discolours his mocking apparel of worn-out patent leather,
administering an interpretative militancy over the old landscape.
For he lashes the worm that passively moves along, crawling,
he loves the female with pink tea-rose blouse and feverish corset, laced-up,
and with the dragging of his old cape lacking universal subjects,
he imposes the ancestral echo of his archaic Parnassian song.
Trembling and oscillating, bordering the plain and its grass,
burlesque demons swing them, dazed, haughty, knock-kneed,
in a draft of circumstantial plaster, filed down or maybe illogical.

With the restlessness of the dejected and overwhelmed storyteller,
a caravan raises up amidst natives and measured airs, in Indian file.
Never destroyed by isolation or the flip side of the medallion,
they meditate within the bark of the ombú that sets them into an inspirational dynamic,
one opposed, by natural theory, to the indigenous figure commemorated.

Dark progressive matter with painful foreboding smile,
between kitchen gardens, cemeteries, mountains, thorny lands, downpours,
such grace takes on the sickly colour of scattered rye
found in the terrifying small-scale governments of Walt Disney.
Else there's an obsession with a sawdust nest thrown together,
insulting the "little old house" made of platinum, with its slaughterhouse buffaloes.

Oh! blanket with luscious fruits on the path to becoming ideas,
in the margins, you outdo every precedent and defining nib
on this book flap, ever so soapy and stubborn, like a yarn ball's tunnel

para ocultar el sentimiento de masa de los robles.
Pero es así este mantel de coronas telúricas y prolíficas,
deleitoso engranaje en cuotidiano fervor antagónico, pintura
mimo de entrega y superstición filosófica,
para mi peinado inédito de Invierno en verificación.

to hide the massive feel of oaks.
But that's how it is, this cloth strewn with earthly prolific wreath,
delightful gear in everyday antagonistic fervour, painting,
tender gesture of surrender and philosophical superstition
for my unprecedented Winter hairstyle, yet to be verified.

*

Los milicianos establecen una raza complementaria, roja, eminente,
desde que trasladaron margaritas de jornadas en cabriolas
lanzadas, de superación en superación, en un esquema de aliento caliente.
Acelerando mi consejo guerrero de antaño, cachorro de león,
voy, en temerosa vestal, entre la marcial ilusión cooperadora metálica,
y el destello militante, imperativo, de mi graciosa familia de ágata.
La crisálida suprema de la sabiduría —Safo inmortal— duele
ensangrentándome las uñas de origen escocés,
cuando mi espalda de misal, desnuda y peregrina de diosa,
recibe un culto de nácar y real cosecha paulatina por tatuaje.
Llenan de frío y brea los zapatos rígidos del cadáver invertido,
el acordeón de las amapolas mutiladas, peludas, lentas,
las señoras ranas de virtud, los lagartos cantores, cocodrilos, de fórmula,
el sapo burgués calenturiento, cetrino, de intención turquesa.
Mariposas con complejo azteca entre la liga-luna
zopilotes atorrantes de portavoz negro por senderos de hambre con obreros
tan pálidos como la cólera.

*

The conscripts set up a race that's parallel, red, eminent,
since they transferred daisies after days of launching cartwheels,
going from overcoming to overcoming, in a diagram of hot breath.
Speeding up my warlike advice from before, lion cub,
I go, fearful vestal virgin, amidst the martial illusions of collaborators in metal,
and the militant, commanding glitter of my elegant agate family.
The supreme chrysalis of wisdom – immortal Sappho – pains me,
covering in blood my fingernails of Scottish origin,
as my back hard as a missal, naked and wandering like that of a goddess,
receives mother-of-pearl worship and gradual royal harvest by tattoo.
With cold and pitch, they fill the rigid shoes of the hanging corpse,
the accordion of the hacked, bristling, slow poppies,
the virtuous lady frogs, the singing lizards, the formulaic crocodiles,
the horny bourgeois toad, greenish-yellow, with intentions of turquoise.
Butterflies with Aztec insecurities under the matchmaker-moon,
good-for-nothing buzzards holding black megaphones on paths to hunger,
as the workers stare pale as cholera.

*

Vivir a la entrada de un documento viejo
que da paletas enlutadas y ráfagas de artillería en carpeta mecánica
para despertar piedras paspadas, plegarias leñosas y jerigonza.
Esteros englobados y embobados, forasteros, largos ríos de salmos veleidosos
de conjugación en permanencia y pompa de imposible y lamento.
El corcel pueblerino acomete rabioso y unísono empujando
el pesado caudal persistente, echado en la honda cola de langosta.
Con el cerebro al revés, dilatado, en hamaca púrpura, ignorante, placentero, inocente,
miro a Dios-Dictador a mis plantas,
el que con barniz vidente, precipitado de smoking y coraza urbana
rompió en pedazos la vorágine de alarde de un penacho.
Cartón de pepas rojas cuyo resumen es la altiplanicie que crepita sus ciclos
sobre lo inmaculado traslúcido en metamorfosis campestre.

*

To live at the entrance of an old document
that gives spadefuls of mourning and bursts of artillery in a mechanical folder,
to awaken cracked stones, wooden prayers and jargon.
Girded and gobsmacked estuaries, foreigners, long rivers of fickle psalms,
of conjugation in stability and impossible pomp and lament.
The provincial steed charges furious and in unison, pushing along
the determined heavy flow, cast into the lobster's tail slingshot.
With brain reversed and delayed, in purple hammock, ignorant, pleasurable, naïve,
I look at the God-Dictator under my soles,
He who with clairvoyant varnish, hasty with dinner jacket and urbane shell
broke to pieces the whirlwind display of a plume.
Carton of red seeds whose summary is the high plateau spluttering its cycles
over immaculate translucence, in rural metamorphosis.

*

Quebradura mineral de esqueleto con estribo,
sementera oxidada ¡*Teotihuacán!* y su bálsamo pétreo con cerillas de granito.
Herreros amanecidos y corpiños que se agrupan, fragua-catacumba y locura,
el bermellón y el gualda más directo templando su licor de asamblea.

Catedral imaginaria para el monstruo, champagne, alforjas
titán sorbedor de vapores, sin fatiga, etapa embrionaria,
cojines altivos para las nuevas rebeliones contrarias.
Sudores de incienso encarnan cizaña y mixtura
y enarcan la anestesia difusa del animal de barro en bungalows.

Perlada es la conciencia del tabernáculo terrestre,
con un esclavo extirpado, decapitado y moneda pueril por ofrenda.

Tubérculo reptante, monaguillo, torrente cirujano, cercena
la abrumadora, inaccesible borrasca de comadre y escoba eufórica.
Espirales de granizo en claro-oscuro de guirnaldas de miel alborotadas
se extasían en el pabellón remoto de los cinco rizos cardinales.
Contemplo el escenario impulsado de fábulas de harina
por el estruendo trepidante de la pólvora verbal de la fortuna.
Entre bruñidas tonalidades escalonadas de malva y heliotropo
murallas y tejados bermejos en sonido y comentario de difuntos,
el bosque preñado que araña y carraspea en augurio
en colaboración con los archipiélagos de castaños que apuntan sombríos los lampadarios.
Les he platicado por acuerdo a las furias aladas del huracán con tenedor
no con la lengua terciada de los cetáceos jorobados de etiqueta y cultura
pero con la lujosa cátedra de mi jardinflor de mujer en todos los pueblos.

*

Mineral fracture of a skeleton with stirrups,
rusty sown field, Teotihuacan! and its rocky balsam with wax tapers of granite.
Blacksmiths at dawn and grouped bodices, catacomb-forge and madness,
the vermilion and most intense gold cooling their liquor of assembly.

Imaginary cathedral for the monster, champagne, saddlebags,
titan absorber of steam without fatigue, embryonic stage,
haughty cushions for new opposing rebellions.
Sweats of incense embody vice and mingling,
and fasten hoops upon the vague anaesthesia of the mud animal in bungalows.

Pearly is the conscience of the earth's tabernacle,
with a slave rooted out and decapitated, a trivial coin given as offering.

Crawling tuber, acolyte, surgeon's torrent of blood, serve to cut off
the overwhelming, inaccessible squall of gossip and euphoric disorder.
Spirals of hail in a chiaroscuro of whirled honey garlands
go into ecstasies on the remote pavilion of five cardinal loops.
I contemplate the scene driven by legends of flour,
by the ear-splitting boom of the verbal gunpowder of fortune.
Between polished staggered tonalities of mallow and heliotrope,
huge walls and light-brown roofs in sound and commentary of the dead,
the pregnant forest scratches and clears its throat in prophecy,
in collaboration with the archipelagos of chestnut trees that take sombre aim at chandeliers.
By agreement I've talked to the winged furies of the hurricane with its bookkeeper,
not in the worn-out language of hunched cetaceans with fancy dress and culture
but in the luxurious professorship of my woman's gardenflower, in every village.

*

Valiente pincel de hacer célebre, proletario-macho-desterrado
fecundas generaciones de amaranto y ponzoña perforada.
Poetas de la concordia y su articulación multitudinaria
calcina granadas de juventud y calavera al relato entregadas.
Imponentes montañas se desgajan en quejumbre borracha
intercalando peñascos de orfeón, cálidos, cárdenos
del carácter enmohecido con musgo eterno a la cintura.
Se multiplican las curvas de las vanguardias cercadas y cercanas
por tostado dolor, lejanas azul-comienzo, precursoras,
umbral y pasto del aloe fraternal.

Se enfrenta el globo-émbolo de estaño a una tétrica mueca cosmogónica;
es que nos acarrea la innúmera cantidad del agua y su dilema orgánico.

Monumentos de vidrio suspendidos, romances de acierto, estupores blancos.
"Futurismo" y canoas, puñal maya-azteca detenido, cerrajero,
en tal ansiedad manejada de rubíes equivalentes.
El relámpago triangulado se yergue arrollador,
trincha la Cruz del Sur que reverbera en sí misma de emergencia.
Gusanos que arrasan la carne de mármol y vigilia.
El grito mundial de "*Buy bonds of war,*"[2] lisonjero,
en la médula de millones de seres deambulando en desborde
con esperanza leve y la fría finura del murciélago libre.

---

[2] Campaña publicitaria que inicia el gobierno norteamericano en 1941 con el fin de que los ciudadanos compraran "Bonos de Guerra" con el fin de recaudar fondos para solventar los gastos militares del país en la Segunda Guerra Mundial, a la cual los Estados Unidos habían ingresado ese año. Se realizaron carteles y diversas formas de publicidad, incluyendo giras artísticas, que promovían la compra de estampillas, discos y diversos productos afiliados a la campaña.

*

Valiant brush that creates fame, proletarian-macho-exile,
fertile generations shot through with amaranth and venom.
Poets of harmony and its mass articulation,
concrete grenades of youth and skull devoted to the tale.
Imposing mountains break off with a drunken groan,
smashing in choired ridges, warm, violet,
with a mouldy character skirted by eternal moss.
The curves of the vanguardias multiply, closed by and close
to dark-brown pain, distant blue-beginning, heralds,
threshold, pasture of fraternal aloe.

The tin balloon-piston faces off against a glum cosmogonical face;
it brings us a countless quantity of water and its organic dilemma.

Monuments of suspended glass, romances that hit the mark, astonishment as target.
"Futurism" and canoes, Mayan-Aztecan dagger stopped, locksmith,
with such anxiety manipulated by equivalent rubies.
The triangulated lightning bolt straightens out, overpowering,
and carves the Southern Cross that reflects on itself, in emergence.
Worms devastate the flesh of marble and vigil.
The worldwide cry "Buy bonds of war",[5] flattering,
is in the marrow of millions of wandering beings spilling forth
with light hope, and the cold daintiness of the free-flying bat.

---

[5] Publicity campaign begun by the United States government in 1941, encouraging citizens to buy "War Bonds" to help cover military costs during the Second World War. The country entered the war that year. Posters and other forms of advertising, including artistic tours, were used to promote the purchase of stamps, albums and other products affiliated with the campaign.

Oda de lodo del banquete escalofriante, de hotel,
su frasco de alcohol refrena el maxilar y la mímica impúdica.
El echarpe soltero de la plaza pública auspicia ceremonias universales;
un tropel de potrancas matizan las drogas de relleno del fenómeno.

Canal suave, rítmico, cuadro de hojas crujientes, recalcitrantes,
patinado, celestial, recortado, solo, característico, antojo, percance intestinal
de una procesión de azucenas traviesas en planteamiento de aviones.
Libro-apóstol aborda la memoria frívola de una oruga con dólares.

Enigma y arboladura de catedrales medioevales, cortina de latidos,
con pestañeos termales bajo el flujo de la Vía Láctea.
Al ataque esponjadas señales luminosas, zorros, puritanos,
melindrosos, cautelosos como aborigen desgraciado, fugitivo.
Difícilmente tomaré ya contacto directo, cobarde, inútil,
de salmuera, con los lares de mis antepasados de cobre y cochayuyo.
Molécula aterida, categórica, aerodinámica, baile
en que giro sin término y polémica impávida o amenazadora.

Ode to mud at the bloodcurdling feast, in a hotel,
its bottle of alcohol letting loose the jaw and shameless mimicry.
The lonely scarf in the public square augurs universal ceremonies;
a horde of fillies complements the drugs omnipresent at the phenomenon.

Gentle and rhythmic canal, picture of crisp and stubborn leaves,
shiny, celestial, jagged, alone, characteristic, yen, intestinal mishap
at a procession of naughty madonna lilies in a blueprint of aeroplanes.
Book-apostle tackles the frivolous memory of a caterpillar with dollars.

Enigma and rigging of mediaeval cathedrals, drape of heartbeats,
with thermal blinks under the Milky Way's flow.
On the attack, springy luminous gestures, foxes, puritans,
contrived, prudent as the unlucky and fugitive aborigine.
With difficulty I'll now make direct contact, lily-livered, useless,
brine-soaked, with the homes of my ancestors, of copper and cochayuyo.[6]
Molecule stiff with cold, resolute, aerodynamic, a dance
in which I spin, endless, within an intrepid or threatening polemic.

---

[6] *cochayuyo*: A large algae with a leathery texture, native to Chile. Sometimes it is translated as "bull kelp".

*

¡Ah! cómo vuelvo a tomar conexión y alarma evocadora de nosotros, celestes,
con los dos cantarinos, estrafalarios, horadados y obsesionantes
campanarios de baluarte que me cobijan defendiéndome:
el prusia nuevo de influencia colectiva y el de profundidad de muchedumbre
orna y ruina perpendicular a las plataformas interrogantes.
Me traspasa, desintegrándome, la sensación oportuna de los rebaños en bautismo.

Lazadas de salamandras hacia abajo, períodos,
arrogancia, exploraciones colgadas de efluvios hacia arriba ubicados, feriados.
Se concibe un jíbaro ahorcándose entre nidada de nardos y marimba.
Troncos, esteros, platanares, cauchales, campiñas que dan alimañas,
helechos clandestinos, cafetales, laxitud desmadejada, exótica, indulgente,
todo estallando como polvorazo entre los renglones lacustres de Claudia Lars.

En las arterias trianguladas del conjunto gramatical y sus polainas,
la truculencia rubicunda apachurra y pregona, agazapada de guantes iguales,
la fauna golosa y la flora de broma pintoresca del vecindario goloso.

*

*

Ah! how I once again set up a connection and evocative warning about us, celestial,
with the two singers, eccentric, perforated and obsessive,
stockaded bell towers that shelter and defend me:
the new Prussia of collective influence and the profundity of the crowd,
adornment and ruin perpendicular to interrogating platforms.
It pierces through, disintegrates me, the convenient sensation of flocks at baptism.

Lasso-snatches downwards of salamanders, periods,
arrogance, explorations hanged from outpourings directed upwards, holidays.
One imagines a jivaro[7] hanged between a clutch of tuberoses and a marimba drum.
Trunks, estuaries, banana plantations, rubber plantations, farmlands that produce bloodsuckers,
clandestine ferns, coffee plantations, fatigued laxity, exotic, indulgent,
everything detonating in a big explosion within the lakeside verses of Claudia Lars.[8]

In the triangulated arteries of the grammatical set-up and its nuisances,
a ruddy aggression, crouched with equivalent gloves, squeezes in and announces
the gluttonous fauna and picturesque comic flora of a gluttonous neighbourhood.

---

[7] *jivaro*: person from a tribe found in northern Peru and eastern Ecuador.
[8] Pseudonym of Carmen Brannon Vega, a Salvadoran poet who was born in Armenia in 1899 and died in San Salvador in 1974. She published several books of poetry between 1934 and 1972.

Las aldeas interrumpen su insomnio y su energía
al tranco del anfibio armado que proyecta geometría
entre colmenas, vacadas, volúmenes y pámpanos gentiles.
Por las comarcas ululantes sus anillos se retratan movidos
y una congoja impresionante de vid que se desangra
lo sigue como lengua de perro cansado entre malezas.
Las encinas inclinan el anca desolada de otros días
cuando la espada de Núñez de Balboa unió dos inmensidades.
Entre cintas de jade surgen fuertes matojos de tezontle oriental,
collares-circundantes de bondad, para mis hombros cenicientos.
Remeros intoxicados con sueño letárgico, extático, chalupas de chanza,
flota nazarena pululan entre obeliscos y surtidores efervescentes, susurrantes.
Un temporal de cables, botes, olas, gaviotas, fragatas, bagaje,
promueve el espasmo sobrenatural que conduce los bueyes al mercado.

*

The villages break off their insomnia and their energy
with long strides of an armed amphibian projecting geometry
amidst beehives, herds of cows, volumes and elegant vineshoots.
Through howling comarcas their rings sketch themselves in movement
and an impressive anguish, that of the vine losing blood,
follows it like a dog's tongue through weeds.
Oaks bend forward the devastated stump of other days
when the sword of Núñez de Balboa[9] brought together two immensities.
Between jade ribbons emerge strong briars made of eastern volcanic rock,
circling-necklaces of kindness for my ash-grey shoulders.
Rowers intoxicated with lethargic dream, ecstatic, canoes of opportunity,
a Nazarene fleet, crowd around the obelisks and the bubbling, murmuring fountains.
A storm of cables, boats, waves, seagulls, frigates, luggage,
provokes the unearthly spasm that leads the oxen to market.

---

[9] *Vasco Núñez de Balboa*: a Spanish conquistador

*

Hundida en un sillón de lirios en vigencia vehemente,
origino una órbita de leyes sociales que se cumplen inmensamente.
Una silueta de sirena espantada, verdosa y traidora
se inclina ante un alacrán naci-fascista con tripas de tijera
y sus senos de cantárida cercan a una paloma invulnerable.
Elaboro la capota arborescente, guijarro de pavor, y su copihue militar.

Los tentaculares montones de nubarrones olímpicos
y su parque imperial graduado, son comidos por el rayo.
Borróse el zagal arrebol dando tregua a las últimas fieras
y al estampido del trueno, igual y consecutivo,
esfumó la televisión partida de jacintos intrusos
por la curiosidad anémica de láudano, del instante.

*

Plunged into a divan of lilies with vehement authority,
I generate an orbit of social laws carried out with thoroughness.
The silhouette of a scared siren, green-coloured traitor,
bows before a Nazi-fascist scorpion with scissor guts,
whose blistered sinuses close in upon an invulnerable dove.
I prepare the arborescent hood, pebble of terror, and its military copihue.[10]

The grasping heaps of Olympian storm clouds
and their imperial commissioned park are swallowed by the lightning bolt.
It wiped out the young rustic afterglow giving truce to the final beasts
and the thunderclap boom, identical and consecutive,
it blotted out the television cracked open by intruding hyacinths
with the anaemic curiosity of laudanum, on the instant.

---

[10] *copihue*: Chilean bell flower.

*

¿Qué mica de comba iluminada, bibliotecaria, prisma del éxtasis,
comenta la imagen doblada de mi rostro marchito?
Y esas colleras monolíticas, velludas, despampanantes,
¿por qué recortan en audaces redondelas fucsias podridas,
trenzas terráqueas con límites rojizos, madreselvas y prostitutas,
discos carmíneos, consejeros personales de lo lúgubre?
Es el bardo que se enreda a la nebulosa de los pistilos,
al matorral y a la conciencia del presente lateral, plateresco,
la leña de lo ido, la insignia de lo incierto definido.
El que atravesó la monotonía abundante y elocuente de los senderos enamorados
sabrá por envolver y nutrir el balcón de los cardenales,
aquella religión de majadas que se ruedan al atardecer
cuando las mujeres se desnudan en síntomas de cursilería,
con pájaros ufanos y flores secas en el búcaro del vientre.

*

Of what little child with luminous skip rope, librarian, ecstatic prism,
does the folded image of my withered face speak?
And why cut those monolithic animal pairs, hairy, spectacular,
into bold rotten circles of fuchsia,
earthly plaits with red boundaries, honeysuckles and whores,
discs of crimson, personal advisers on melancholy?
It's the bard who tangles up the vagueness of pistils,
the scrubland and the consciousness of a sidelong ornamental present,
the firewood of what's past and the emblem of defined uncertainty.
He who crossed through the abundant and eloquent monotony of loving paths
will know after enveloping and nourishing the balcony of cardinals
about that religion of herds that roam about at dusk,
when the women undress with symptoms of poor taste,
vain birds and dry flowers in the clay pots of their bellies.

*

Un parpadeo de tinta escolar, se abre discontinuo, loco, efusivo.
Luciérnagas acompañan la arrogancia temperamental
del abejorro rumoroso, mercader de la conquista incendiada del pirata.
A lo lejos un escuadrón de fiesta popular
abriga la acuarela crepuscular de la caleta y sus mendrugos.
Arroyos con piyamas matinales en corolario feliz, plasmados,
o ramazones de substancia gemebunda de nenúfares en desvelo.
Desarticulando los pulmones agrícolas del maíz en lámpara de números,
y el dorso de imprenta de sus terrenales figuras-bestias,
un ocre de edades y de castas amotinándose en sus muletas patinadas.
Taller de pétalos de bronce —esmeraldinos—, que se funden,
cardales graves de ciudades que oscilan, romería póstuma, portada,
estoicas tembladeras, arquetipo de picaflores, (hilo),
ya inventados en la suerte sin determinación
que extravía el acento singular de toda transparencia.

*

A flicker of ink from schooldays, it opens, discontinuous, mad, effusive.
Fireflies accompany the temperamental arrogance
of the murmuring bumblebee, trader of the pirate's burning conquest.
In the distance, a squadron from the neighbourhood party
shelters the dusky watercolour of the little cove and its crusts.
Streams with morning pyjamas as happy corollary, on the record,
or antlers with the howling substance of insomniac water lilies.
Taking apart the agricultural lungs of corn under a lamp of numbers,
and the printer's overleaf with its earthly figure-beasts,
an ochre of ages and classes rising up on their skidding crutches.
Workshop of bronze petals – emerald – that melt together,
grave thistle fields in oscillating cities, posthumous pilgrimage, book cover,
stoic shaking fits, archetype of hummingbirds (thread),
now invented in the destiny without resolve
that leads astray the unique accent of every transparency.

*

Acuosa elipse de revueltas calidades amontonando cráneos,
resbaladiza, salpicada, diabólica, entonada, tabique-azotea,
remolacha boreal, azucena, miga de pan, flautas australes y… doctrina,
contra la hojalata distinta, cada vez más etérea y "arrebolada."
Refresco mi túnica sacerdotal y mi pensamiento de palo de rosa,
para contemplar ociosa la florecida aurora del sentido común con zanahoria.
Pero fulgores desencadenados nos precipitan en caldera a sepias insurgentes,
por un aterciopelado fulgor esterilizado, mulato, resonante,
de jugosa pulpa amatista de pantano impudente, hinchado, granadero.
Veleros encadenados, caseríos achatados, suplicios, nichos, idilios
pintados en la mejilla blanda de los héroes y sus amuletos de cacao.

*

Aqueous ellipse of jumbled qualities heaping up skulls,
slippery and splattered, devilish, in tune, partition-rooftop,
northern beetroot, madonna lily, breadcrumb, southern flutes and… doctrine,
against the distinct corrugated iron, ever more ethereal and "red".
I freshen my sacerdotal robe and my thought of rosewood,
to meditate at leisure on the blossoming dawn of common sense with carrot.
But unleashed glows hasten us in a furnace towards insurgent sepias,
through a sterilised velvet glow, mulatto, resonant,
like the juicy amethyst pulp of a brazen swamp, pompous, grenadier.
Chained sailboats, flattened country houses, tortures, niches, idylls
painted on the tender cheek of heroes and their worthless amulets.

*

La floresta uniforme, tendida, morada de prófugos,
cruzada de sorpresas tenebrosas y quejas de tiempo en la felpa nocturna,
posesionada de su arbitraria y magna importancia carnicera.
La jefatura imponente de potros-toros majestuosos en algazara,
sin control, chapotean en charcos elementales de pezuña y mandíbula.
Atardece en absoluta calma prodigiosa, ovalado-emancipado,
mientras la lupa cincela el galope de estrépito con lazarillo, báculo
de los muertos ateos de la roñosería en chinelas de abrigo.
Me rodea un tenaz círculo de fuego que afeita, holgazán,
la inmensa noche aposentada sobre el espíritu pujante en investigación,
anegado y atónito en brote de lenguaje y autopsia rokhiana.
Baltimore,[3] cuna y martillo, serpentina del verso forjador,
parpadeante de lentejuelas, clamores, ballenas y zumbido de vampiros.
Siempre hoscas porciones de pariente de linaza que saludan
a sus albañiles agoreros, y pasan ladrando enfurecidos.

---

[3] "Baltimore, cuna y martillo" hace referencia a la celebración en esa ciudad-puerto el 20 de agosto de 1866, tras varias huelgas y protestas a lo largo del siglo XIX en Estados Unidos, de un gran Congreso Obrero, en el cual los trabajadores deciden abandonar los partidos burgueses y organizar el Partido Nacional Obrero.

*

Unvaried forest, stretched out, dwelling of fugitives,
shot through with menacing surprises and complaints of time, in nocturnal plush,
possessed of its arbitrary and supreme butcher's importance.
Fearsome leadership of majestic colt-bulls in uproar,
out of control, splashing in elemental puddles of hoof and jaw.
It grows dark with the absolute calm of miracle, oval-emancipated,
as the magnifying glass discerns the tumultuous gallop with guide, walking stick,
of atheist corpses, of filthiness in protective slippers.
A tenacious circle of fire surrounds and brushes against me, idler,
immense night lodged in the forceful investigating spirit,
flooded and astounded by an outbreak of language and Rokhian autopsy.
Baltimore, cradle and hammer,[11] streamer of forging verse,
twinkles with spangles, cries, whales, buzz of vampires.
Surly portions of flaxseed relatives forever greet
their prophetic builders, and pass by barking in rage.

---

[11] "Baltimore, cradle and hammer" refers to the celebration in the port-city on 20 August 1866, after many strikes and protest throughout the 19th century in the United States. At a great Workers' Congress, labourers decided to abandon the bourgeois parties and organise the National Labour Union.

*

Extrañada, solemne, confiada, mi casco de naranja latina
sobre el océano amado-ártico-profundo enciende su cigarrillo de taberna.
Imperativo, extraordinario, luminoso, tranquilo en sus anteojos,
la golondrina tensa lo perfila y lo disipa entre páginas convexas de escamas, en pedrería
Se avecinan los rumores de cerveza del tropico, los dátiles,
conducidos en lontananza diagonal, encorvando las clásicas reses,
taza del beso de las costas "bonitas," ultramarinas de Isa Caraballo[24] y sus higueras.
Del balanceo en zozobra salimos verdi-dorados en ascuas,
al lanza-aullido marinero, americano, de: ¡Tierra!
Batido en todas las corrientes del Caribe y sus ciervos retintos
un juguete final, escarabajo de una sobra de cantares
navaja, baíle, sombrilla, algas, carroñas y velámenes.

*

Puzzled, solemn, trusting, my hull of Latin American orange
on the deep-dear-arctic sea lights a cigarette in the bar.
Imperative, extraordinary, luminous, calm through binoculars,
the tense swallow appears and dissolves amidst convex pages of scales, bejewelled.
Murmurs approach about beer in the tropics, about dates,
ushered in from a diagonal, the classic cattle bent over,
mug with the kiss of "pretty" ultramarine coasts, Isa Caraballo* and her fig trees.
Swaying near-to-capsize we depart, greenish-gold, on edge,
to a sailor's lance-howl, American: *Land!*
Beaten against each of the Caribbean's currents and its ink-black stags,
a final plaything, scarab of excess songs,
blade, dance, sunshade, algae, carrion and sails.

* *Isa Caraballo*: A Cuban writer, later disappeared, who focused on political subjects.

*

Fontana de topacios la cuchilla civil de un estanque…
él está turbio con álgebras de percal angusto, de época,
así su faz sumergida por la carcoma de un engaño distante.
¡Oh! perforada y trajinante catarata de espuma, pasadizo tenebroso,
que mezcla, a la deriva, el estallido de un rencor que ha deslucido
la severa canción desvanecida de mi cabello de entonces entre sus manos.
Muchos desembocan como camarones azorados, tordillos, con coletazo empalidecido
al mostrenco líquido entrando a sus riberas de alfileres,
mas yo abundo frente a la pálida trasnochada, amarillenta,
velada de blondas de Venecia y copias postreras de ánimas.
Ya este trino no es mi clima sino el de todos:
demacrado, tierno, diurno, perfecto, tabaco, perejil, emblema,
con salpicaduras de gelatinosos cerotes al nacer, ubres,
jirones rumiantes y aventureros como la tiza del circo.
El cascarón está en la partícula más nítida, (cántaro y delantal),
con deseado tañido de lo casto por capullo y persiana transparente.

*

Spring of topazes the civilian blade of a pond…
he's murky with algebras of narrow calico, of the age,
thus is his face sunk by the anxiety of a far-off deception.
Oh! punctured and bustling waterfall of foam, sinister passage,
that mixes in, drifting, the burst of a resentment dulling
the severe faded song of my hair from back then in his hands.
Many wash up like stunned shrimp, dapple horses with enfeebled tail flick,
in the rootless liquid that enters its riverbanks of spikes,
else I abound before the pale, sleepless, sallow
evening of Venice blondes and final copies of souls in purgatory.
Now this trill is no longer my climate but that of all:
gaunt, tender, daytime, perfect, tobacco, parsley, emblem,
with splashes of jellied wax at birth, udders,
ruminant adventurous shreds like circus chalk.
The eggshell is within the most clearly defined particle (jug and apron),
with desirous tolling of the chaste for the bud and transparent blind.

*

La crudeza ácida, polifacética, que atesora espanto y labor,
todo lo insinúa empapándolo con abrazo y blasfemia de feria.
No sé si entre sus válvulas hay arcilla o légamo o nada.
¿Qué brújula tiene la epidermis del brazalete matutino?
¿Esas frágiles corolas para el tacto floreal, nuboso y terco,
laberinto convulsivo, disparejo, barroco, comunicante,
melódico connubio contradiciéndose creyente?
Acrobacia de ópalos con anarquizado polen gigante conspirando, remembranza,
hábito del breviario, crisol en ramas plomizas y morfina.
Zancadilla brusca, versículo, costumbre, herrajes, fracaso
maravillosamente captado en sus estigmas, la sabandija
impulsada y entroncada por azar de pesadilla
a la brujería lamentable de escapulario, servilleta y hormiga.

*

The acid multifaceted rawness that stockpiles terror and work:
everything hints at it, saturates it with hugs and market day profanity.
I don't know if between its valves there's clay or mud, or nothing.
What compass does the skin of the morning's bangle have?
Those fragile corollas for the blossoming, cloudy, stubborn touch,
convulsive labyrinth, uneven, baroque, communicating,
melodic marriage that contradicts itself, in belief?
Acrobatics of opals with giant anarchic pollen, conspiring, remembrance,
habit of the breviary, crucible in lead and morphine branches.
Abrupt trip, verse, habit, ironworks, failure,
marvellously captured in its stigmas, the louse
set moving and connected by chance of nightmare
to the pathetic witchcraft of the scapulary, napkin, ant.

*

El ruboroso "piélago" agita su jugo de azúcar acibarada, crespo, integral,
tabaquera de bucanero tremante en la amistad, superando su acción esplendorosa.
Conjuga: camarada callampa, camarada culebra y blanca,
camarada Venus, pues, a jugar la primera y oficial encantadora
virgen de azufre desprendida desde la barbarie.
¡Ah! dicen, es el mar, malhechor rebelde,
yo, sin galeras lo veo atento, cercado, apenas amedrentado y grávido
entre las dunas de la libertad y del fragor de Goya de la espera sin nombre y con antorchas.
Altímetro donde la carta solar airea, entre azahares la melena del poema,
el linaje de su guardarropas obstinado sobre las nubaredas de cera.
Un yo abierto vigoriza una fuente nítida,
entre las cenizas coros artificiales hechos de linternas,
sudor y zarzal que empuña el advenimiento de las máscaras, bujías,
los grises de la pelusa sensitiva en la falda áspera guarnecida
de altares con redes y eclipses entretejidos.

*

The blushing "deep sea" shakes its bitter sugar juice, curled, whole,
the buccaneer's tobacco pouch trembling in friendship, surpassing his brilliant actions.
Conjugate: shantytown comrade, white snake comrade,
Venus comrade, and thus, to play the first and official enchanter,
virgin of brimstone emitted since the stone age.
Ah! they say, it's the sea, rebellious delinquent.
I, without galleys, view it attentively, enclosed, just barely scared and pregnant,
amidst dunes of liberty and Goya's clamour for a wait without name, with torches.
Altimeter where the sun's chart gets some air, the poem's long tresses amidst orange blossoms,
the pedigree of its wardrobe stubborn over gathering wax clouds.
An open self gives vigour to a clear source
amidst ashen artificial choirs made of lanterns,
sweat and brambles that seize the just-arrived masks, candlesticks,
greys of sensitive fluff on the rough adorned cloth
of altars with nets and eclipses, intertwined.

*

El va y ven instrumental de los ventarrones asesinos
encauza vacíos con corderos deudos en exceso zambullidos en encajes caminantes
sobre filtros combatidos y combativos por correo y cárcel.
Esas ventoleras eran las que se me prendían a la nuca adolescente
y el caos hacíame hilvanar cosas de misterio, naipe y tormenta.
Desbaratábanse los sopores, atributo de la siesta pastora,
el animal colonizador moría atrás con sus esbirros,
malhumorado, entre tules viscosos, mulas, proyectiles,
y la geografía montañosa y volcánica a la espalda,
en los murallones ponían el escalofrío de las arañas.
Cuevas y prados usurpadores corrían al destierro,
ramalazos y graznidos de lechuzas
remolcando enormes lanchones, espadas, braseros, bodegas,
entre los impulsos del vino, y las perdices mimosas que se cuelgan.

*

The instrumental coming and going of killer gales
channels abysses with lamb kin in excess dives, in wandering lace,
over filters combated and combative by post and prison.
Those blasts of wind were the ones to dress the back of my adolescent neck,
and the chaos made me stitch together things of mystery, playing card and storm.
They shattered to pieces the drowsiness, attribute of the shepherd's siesta,
the colonising animal ill-humoured, died some way back with its thugs,
amidst sticky tulles, mules and projectiles,
a mountainous volcanic geography behind,
and into the great walls they put the shiver of spiders.
Usurping caves and meadows ran towards exile,
gusts and squawks of owls
towing enormous launches, swords, braziers, cellars,
amidst impulses of wine and hanging quail mimosas.

*

Las ruecas con su dulzor femenino de esencia cantarina[1]
adquieren cirios discretos en el candor del huerto espectador.
El concho del vaso de horchata, en la sima, rueda con índice,
a favor de los remansos, ermitaño, en lo alto de la pasión;
atletas de pechos esporádicos o aspirando a una columna grácil,
intolerante y pisoteando la línea divisoria y sus abejas legendarias.

Marx y la grandiosa cabalgata de sus columnas,
nos descubrió la ruta-bandera del juramento,
y la herradura del Minotauro triunfador,
nos puso el pulso sobre las orfandades heridas.
Soldados de hallazgo dan palmazos enardecidos
a lo rocoso en las muñecas del templo con gallo y Cancerbero.
Zumbador del aire, radiante, enyuga las celosías al hallar tu excelso lecho
clasificándote sobre sollozos soberbios e impura cóncava palanca.

*

Spinning wheels with their feminine gentleness of melodious essence
acquire modest candles in the sincerity of the garden observer.
What's left of the glass of horchata,[12] in the chasm, wheel with pointer,
favours quiet places, hermit, at the height of passion;
athletes with chests that are sporadic or aspire to graceful columns,
intolerant and trampling the dividing line and its legendary bees.

Marx and the grand parade of his columns
showed us the route-banner of the oath,
and the horseshoe of the triumphant Minotaur
led our hearts to beat with wounded orphanages.
Soldiers of discovery give burning slaps
to stony dolls of the temple with rooster and Cerberus.
That which hums in the air, radiant, yokes its jealousies upon finding your sublime bed,
granting you a place over arrogant sobs and the impurity of hollow leverage.

---

[12] *horchata*: rice milk

*

En negros y tenebrosos tijerales de laurel, hacha y brillo,
donde la nube cuaja bombones, remiendos y desparramadas fantasías,
Guatemala la dulce, la tímida capital orquestal como su pena,
alarga su vestido democrático en profecía de acueducto venerable.
Puritanos de erotismo con cercos de fragua y locomotoras ondinas,
en tajos de crimen, cuello y muslos sacramentales, mal agüero,
arpegio respetable de indígenas petrificados con glándulas de alquitrán.
Me fusiono al oscuro melodrama de los leñadores septentrionales.
El suceder de los damascos alados, conmovidos: raso santo,
clarín, aromos, jazmín y destellos habituales,
fumarolas y cáscaras livianas, convulsión,
argumentando en definitiva la clave del oporto festivo
contra el ramo de líquenes enfermos por sarcasmo y narcótico
sin paralelo entre los ojos.

*

Amidst gloomy black laurel beams, axe and shine,
where candies, patches, scattered fantasies clot within smoke,
Guatemala the gentle, shy capital as orchestral as its grief
stretches out its democratic garb as prophecy of a venerable aqueduct.
Puritans of eroticism enclosed by furnaces and undine locomotives,
in slashes of crime, sacramental neck and thighs, bad omens,
respectable indigenous arpeggio petrified by glands of pitch.
I fuse with the dark melodrama of northern woodcutters.
The unfolding events of winged, soul-stirred apricot trees: holy satin,
bugle, acacias, jasmine and rhythmic glints,
plumes from volcanic vents and insubstantial husks, convulsion,
arguing, in short, the musical key of festive port wine
against the bouquet of lichens sick from sarcasm, and narcotic
without parallel between the eyes.

*

Larga conversación hueca bajo los tilos de balcones rosados de rubor,
que desmenuzan alburas y obsidianas en danza lujuriosa,
seleccionadas por la acrisolada escarcha vertiginosa y general.
Los mirtos colgaron, sensuales, las enaguas doncellas del estío
en los alambres del confabulado elemento-minero de litoral.
Una hoz pura y resonadora me cubre como en oro de episodios,
reverencio con dignidad penetrante la novela de jarcias de la luna y la raíz del símbolo.
Flor y fruto me embriagan la respiración cautiva-ánfora,
encumbrada y alzada hasta quedar amada de los espacios ilustrados.
Omnipotentes combinados de alegorías, proyecciones,
dejan que la mirada concreta abarque la sierra como testigo virgiliano,
que, humanizada, mece en dulces brazos familiares
la almohada del niño poderoso del austro.
Desde mi corazón búho y primitivo, Amatitlán en su agujero
arranca, airosa, una gardenia estremecida e intérprete.

*

Long empty conversation under lime trees, next to balconies rosy with shame,
crumbling whitenesses and obsidians in lustful dance,
selected by a dizzying, expansive purified frost.
The myrtles hung, sensual, petticoat maidens of summer,
from the wire of the conspired miner-section of coast.
A pure, resounding sickle bathes me as in the gold of episodes,
and I revere with piercing dignity the novel of the moon's rigging and symbol's root.
Flower and fruit intoxicate my breathing prisoner-amphora,
raised up and elevated until it's loved by enlightened spaces.
All-powerful combinations of allegories, results,
let the concrete gaze take in as Virgilian witness the mountain range
which, humanised, rocks in sweet familiar arms,
a pillow for that powerful boy-child, the south wind.
From my recluse and primitive heart, Amatitlán in its hole
yanks up, with grace, the shivering interpreter of a gardenia.

*

Acomodada a sus pruebas de aceite o carbón redentor,
tañía yo la yedra-antena de un incontenible ascenso cilíndrico.
Álamos-limoneros, que movían en bruto cabelleras almidonadas y corniza,
organizaban en los confines potreros inundados:
era la defensa inerte contra la bruma de Abril y sus arpas navegantes.
Un plateado ladrón análogo al fango, blanco de llave, de candado como el alma del Popol-Buh,
se apretó frente al semi sombrío de las colinas cristianas,
ya engalanadas de sermón máximo-católico perverso (carretas, clientela)
y vendimias de tumulto dionysíaco y sátira.
Las enredaderas cubrían y recalcaban hongos inefables
con sombrero de copa anárquico y corbata de relieve infernal.
Un resabio pizarra, esbelto, de tono subido, confuso, árido,
saboreando mariscos y moluscos de estilo con oráculo patriotero de ajenjo
entre el comercio de los fuselajes en peregrinación.

*

Used to their tests for redeeming oil or coal,
I strummed the ivy-antenna of an irrepressible cylindrical ascent.
Poplar-lemon trees, that moved as rough starched heads of hair, and cherry dogwoods,
organised at the flooded boundaries of pastures:
it was an unmoving defence against the fog of April and its seafaring harps.
A silvery thief analogous to the mud, white in key and lock as the soul of the Popol Vuh,
squeezed himself before the semi-darkness of the Christian hills,
now adorned with perverse supreme-Catholic sermons (wagons, trade)
and harvests of Dionysian, satirical riot.
The vines covered up and emphasised indescribable mushrooms
with hats of anarchic crown and diabolically stamped ties.
A slate aftertaste, elegant, with intense tone, confusing, arid,
savouring fancy shellfish and molluscs with absinthe's jingoistic oracle,
amidst the business of fuselages on pilgrimage.

*

Café, delito agri-dulce y escarlata, coraje, examen, sigilo,
pequeño nudo y reto contagioso y desafiante olfato, opio, sardinas,
sobre sofocadas bocas, malignas, de azafrán y tortilla flaca.
Las palmeras chasquean, villanas, su látigo y sus ardillas,
tiemblo ante el capricho del acontecer venidero, como resurgiendo despavorida,
y sigo las curvas de las ninfas sencillas, de ámbar, dúctiles,
ensimismadas, envolviéndose, evaporadas, litúrgicas,
en sedas puras que rasgan en descomunal secreto su balbuceo abrasado.
Sedimentos reminiscentes y olorosos a eucalipto mojado
densificándose para el aterrizaje mañanero y sus estadios
y tú, Pablo, en la espiral única conmigo;
Whitman, de Rokha, Maiakovsky, toda la fronda social florida fructificada.
Acuarium lacerado de belleza salvaje, diáfano, retablo
que soterra y escarba espectros temporales
en la barriga de un racimo de uvas en tortura, agobiadas,
soleadas y envejecidas al rescoldo monstruoso del prejuicio.

*

Café, bittersweet scarlet crime, rage, test, stealth,
small knot and contagious threat and defiant smell, opium, sardines,
over suffocated mouths, evil, of saffron and thin tortilla.
The palm trees click, villains, their whip and their squirrels.
I tremble before the whim of the coming event, as if emerging again with terror,
and I follow the curves of simple nymphs, of amber, malleable,
daydreaming, wrapped up in themselves, evanescent, liturgical,
in pure silks that rip in colossal secrecy their burning stammer.
Sediments reminiscent and fragrant of wet eucalyptus
growing dense for the early-morning landing and its stages,
and you, Pablo, in the unique spiral with me;
Whitman, de Rokha, Mayakovsky, the whole social foliage flowering, bearing fruit.
Injured aquarium of savage beauty, translucent, altarpiece
that buries and digs up temporal spectres
in the belly of a cluster of grapes feeling tortured, overwhelmed,
sunny and aged by the monstrous ember of prejudice.

*

Al tránsito de sembradura alfombrada por mi andar seguro cristalino,
contesta la cabritilla como deslumbramiento de trigos simultáneos-sombreados,
y los lagares de intangible fluir calcomaníaco.
Las trombas allá se vienen encima con mecánicos presentimientos,
(desaliños primitivos del diluvio), todo para la niña cándida de canastillo galante,
que inventó su amargura colegiala con rodilla limón y trofeo.
Carátula con título fosfórico y yelmo, testamento
en anaquel olvidado o en ropero de caoba modelo donde da eco un balido
que suspira por una civilización vegetal proclamada en los libros.
Esbozo el llano con ceño conductor, de rebanada expansiva,
arrepintiéndome del miraje al soslayo de lo devoto ceroteado en botón.
A las romerías de aletargados cisnes, laderas exiguas
dan laguna y el reflejo de las ondas porosas, inconexas, jesuitas los despluma;
una sílaba estridente se disuelve en los vistosos plisados angostos
del caprichoso abanico con el limo parasitario que sonríe a los átomos.

*

In the transit of sowing carpeted by my sure diamond clear walk,
the calfskin replies like the glint of simultaneous-shaded wheat,
and the winepresses with an intangible carbon-copied flow.
The torrents there plunge down with mechanical premonitions,
(primeval carelessness of the deluge), all for the naïve girl with charming basket,
who invented her schoolgirl bitterness with lemon knees and trophy.
Stage with phosphoric title and helmet, testament
on a forgotten shelf or in a mahogany-design wardrobe where a bleat echoes
sighing for some vegetal civilisation proclaimed in books.
With conductor's scowl, I sketch out the plains, an expansive slab,
while regretting the sidelong mirage of the pious with waxed badge.
To the religious pilgrimages with drowsy swans, the scant hillsides
offer a lake plucked by the reflections of porous, disjointed, Jesuit waves;
a strident syllable dissolves in the spectacular narrow pleats
of the capricious fan with parasitic mud that smiles at atoms.

*

El contacto dual de los aerolitos prófugos, (cascadas y cantigas rosas),
utilizando va su fiebre fértil en otras latitudes de desastre y horquilla.
Cae una gota de sangre con pimienta y su germen quimérico
sobre el cadalso lívido del periódico que gesta un ratón
como si desmantelara la meseta montada, uniforme,
y sus pedazos de andrajo en surco de asnos y camellos.
Poseo piel de polvera de dama-duende con camafeo que ama en danza de cierzos
entre la elevación híbrida donde algunas hebras rayaban el alba,
separadas de la membranosa manada alegórica de hoy
sufriente entre los azulejos confundidos del antifaz, el zócalo de un madero cruzado.
Otra botella por cigüeña grita realización a ansiedad pictórica;
la acústica del gimnasio incorpora su cilindro y su betún;
en el plato de greda cosmopolita del paladar queda la nada;
Angélica Arenal[4] compone los repollos y las lechugas de todas las huertas del mundo.

---

[4] Angélica Arenal, última esposa, desde 1937, del pintor muralista mexicano David Alfaro Siqueiros, hasta la muerte de éste en 1972. Escribió el libro *Vida y obra de David Alfaro Siqueiros* (México: Fondo de Cultura Económica, 1975).

*

The dual contact of fugitive meteorites (pink cascades and hymns),
make good use, sending fertile fever into other latitudes, of disaster and pitchfork.
A drop of blood falls with pepper and its chimerical germ
onto the pale scaffold of the newspaper, gestating a rat
as if dismantling the mounted meseta, uniform,
and its pieces of rag within a furrow of asses and camels.
I possess skin of powder compact, of lady-leprechaun with cameo who loves in a dance of
      northern winds
amidst the hybrid elevation where some threads frayed from day,
separated from today's allegorical membranous mob
suffering amidst the confused mask tiles, the main square with wood cross.
Another bottle by stork shouts fulfilment to pictorial anxiety;
the gym acoustics incorporate its cylinder and its tar;
on the cosmopolitan clay plate of the palate is left nothingness;
Angélica Arenal[13] composes cabbages and lettuces for all the world's vegetable gardens.

---

[13] Angélica Arenal was the last wife of the Mexican muralist painter David Alfaro Siqueiros, from 1937 until his death in 1972. She wrote the book *Life and Work of David Alfaro Siqueiros* (Mexico City: Fondo de Cultura Económica, 1975).

*

Con ojo absorto, vaso y plumas de cordura perpetua,
el yo revienta sus zafiros de abstracción en pelotón y sin aviso,
mientras el vuelo escribe estrofas.
Siempre el jardín espinudo, vertebrado, yermo, idéntico en la voluntad ardida,
(balde entre los balnearios abiertos de la madrugada y sus barrancas),
o las glorietas y criptas transitorias de los mártires.
Otra instancia a otra similar, atormentada de vallados,
otro dolor desencajado, inmortal, desvencijado,
todo fundido en lo extranjero del árido problema desgranado.
¡Ventisqueros! y una mancha tan extraña, cieno sinuoso, inabarcable,
posiblemente reliquias ardorosas, intersticios, privilegios,
donde la misión de Bolívar, holló los fértiles extremos,
nunca alimentando de tortugas la frase que se extingue en peldaños
sino el incendio permanente que ordena lo invisible.

*

With absorbed eye, drinking glass and ever-sane quill,
the self bursts forth as firing squad, with its sapphires of abstraction, without warning,
and the flight writes verses.
Forever a prickly, spiky, uncultivated garden, constant in its burning will
(a bucket amidst open seaside resorts at early morning and their cliffs),
or the transitory arbours and crypts of martyrs.
Another petition then another similar, tortured by fences,
another dislocated, undying, wobbly grief,
all merged in the foreignness of the arid problem taken from its husk.
Snowdrifts! and a stain so peculiar, devious mire, boundless,
possibly fervent relics, interstices, privileges,
where Bolívar's mission treads the fertile extremes,
providing not nourishment at a turtle's pace, the phrase extinguished goal by goal,
but rather that permanent fire which gives order to the invisible.

*

En mis entrañas dormían los ocasos desintegrados al rococó
se asimilaban los fogones de las bocinas de los motores
y las cabalgaduras de encanto escribieron su leyenda.
Ahora es este desborde que inunda y aletarga como hornacina; los obispos
alrededor de rimas de género y tórtolas oscuras en melodía,
y modulación en penumbra.
Cocoteros de reposo abrigados por mortecinos resplandores,
en ornamentación primorosa, talar, hinojo, sombrero,
selva, cadenciosa selva, esmerilada, tarjeta, olivares y emparrados
aureola fluida, poderosa, tajaduras envenenadas, arrugas,
y por la lava nocturna singulares regueros helados y elásticos, hilando
y deshilvanando su difuso ovillo oculto, su lente fatal, pegajoso,
selva grandilocuente, selva de selva, reiterada, jubilosa, ilusoria…

*

Within my insides there slumbered fractured rococo sunsets
resembling bonfires of engine klaxons,
as enchanted horses wrote their legend.
Now is this spilling-over that floods and produces languor like an alcove; bishops
surrounding typical rhymes and dark turtledoves in tune,
and modulation from the shadows.
Coconut palms at rest sheathed by faint radiances,
in skilful adornment, chop down, fennel, hat,
forest, rhythmic forest, polished, card, olive groves and arbours,
fluid aura, powerful, slashes of poison, wrinkles,
and throughout the nocturnal lava, odd tracks, frozen and elastic, ravelling
and unravelling their dim hidden ball of thread, their fatal lens, sticky,
bombastic forest, forest of forest, repeating, jubilant, illusory…

*

Baladas de ganados legales inquietos, vagabundos balidos tardíos,
mas limbo de torres épicas, radiantes de pulsera diplomática,
"deleitoso" manantial de bólido en almíbar de pic-nic cómico,
de estallante electricidad y poderío, magnánimo, galán báquico,
en donde querubes en camisa se desentumedecen amodorrados.
La lluvia crepita interfundiendo la cal de los portales solariegos,
echando a volar gorriones y guitarras de clase-media y poesía.
Ya el toro rojo, ventrudo, caluroso y amoroso entre habichuelas
hace vagabundear las penas desconsoladas de la espiga privada.
¡Oh! pulpo sonámbulo, el universo demuestra a los polichinelas del camino
que los Narcisos hinchados de fronda intelectual y umbroso significado son reales.
Veleros desenfrenados, ignotos cancelan quebrantos de ausencia
al relumbrón que adopta y acepta su acento deletéreo, ideal,
por quebrados claustros, apios y sepulcros lóbregos rielando
en conveniente pereza de teclado diluido
por el cortinaje de aluviones en predominio superpuesto y aberrante.

*

Ballads of restless legal cattle, bleating tardy vagabonds,
or else limbo of epic towers, radiant from diplomatic wristbands,
"delightful" spring of meteorites in the syrup of a comic picnic,
of explosive electricity and power, magnanimous, a bacchic ladies' man,
where cherubs in shirts drowsily loosen up.
The rain sizzles, fusing with the whitewash of ancient entrance halls,
making fly the sparrows and the guitars of middle-class and poetry.
Now the red bull, potbellied, hot and amorous amidst kidney beans,
sets wandering the inconsolable sorrows of the deprived sprig.
Oh! sleepwalking octopus, the universe demonstrates to the punchinellos along the way
that the conceited Narcissi of intellectual foliage and shady significance are real.
Unknown, runaway sailboats pay for breakdowns of absence
to the show-off that adopts and accepts his lethal, ideal accent,
through broken cloisters, celeries, gloomy tombs shimmering
in the convenient sloth of the dissolved keyboard,
through the curtain of flooding in superimposed, aberrant predominance.

*

Las cejas de arroz del cedro y sus tañidos hierven
imitando un choapino agrandado en jeroglíficos de Aristóteles.
Plumillas mágicas se resarcían cascabeleando pelirrojas,
cuando lo diáfano desdeñó su pentagrama caudillo… (caserones
tachonados de reverencias de vidriería de sanatorio, lavada,
variada por la brisa circundante y su aguijón opulento).
Injertos de duraznos caballeros o hipopótamos de frescura
y recipientes donde amanecen las hadas de estos parajes solitarios sin gato.
Corredor, halo de algo, hacinamiento en las cimas colmadas, diluido por puñados de tulipanes,
programa maestro, de avellana para la boina de un títere facultativo.
Las campesinas de manzana evidencian el cuarzo de su cuerpo
en un pozo sin pérgola, sin nodriza, con mirra, ciruelas y cerezas
en un soberbio efecto laxo de inocente nostalgia y pantorrilla.

*

The brows of cedar rice and their pealing as they boil
mimic an expanding wool mat with Aristotle's hieroglyphs.
Magic nib pens sought compensation, taking in redheads
when the diaphanous scorned its tyrant of music paper… (big houses
studded with devotions from the shop windows of a sanatorium, rinsed,
varied by the surrounding breeze and its sumptuous sting).
Grafts of chivalrous peaches or fresh hippopotami
and vessels where the fairies of such lonely spots, without cats, awaken.
Passage, halo of something, overcrowding at the crammed peaks, diluted by fistfuls of tulips,
master plan, with hazelnut for the beret of a medical puppet.
The applelike peasant women show off the quartz of their bodies
in a well without pergola, without nursemaid, with myrrh, plums and cherries,
in a proud relaxed effect full of innocent nostalgia and lower leg.

*

Cintas brillantes, vallas, cebollas, verano de maizales y cerdos,
impostura lagunera sin realidad, equívoca, sorbete de fraile,
y el espejismo múltiple-mitológico, de improvisada configuración y euritmia.
Y la presencia de la blusa irreal y el viejo pelo hermético del piloto de níquel:
un enigma de bambú sentado al borde de una tumba y su acróstico.
¡Resbalar por praderas de porcelana, acuáticas, hacia la parva inclinada
junto a una pajarera de horda, de arbitraria y ruidosa fama!
El mosquito bronceado y las chozuelas de espinas que se desgarran
en respuesta de verbo-víboras sucediéndose en los linderos de choque.
Me baño, exploradora, en la perplejidad de lo inaudito,
en aquella claridad amenazada y cauce ruiseñor de campamento
de su mismo tesoro taumaturgo, torrencial, inadvertido,
hacia las etapas y los arrecifes de temperatura y métodos desconocidos.

*

Shining ribbons, fences, onions, summer of cornfields and pigs,
imposter lake without reality, erroneous, friar's sherbet
and the multiple-mythological mirage of improvised configuration and eurhythmics.
And the presence of the unreal blouse, and the old inscrutable hair of the nickel pilot:
an enigma of bamboo sitting beside a tomb and its acrostic.
To slide through ivory meadows, aquatic, towards the slope of unthreshed grain
next to an aviary with its flock of random and noisy fame!
The sun-kissed mosquito and the prickly little huts that come apart
in response to verb-vipers chasing each other over boundaries of collision.
I bathe, explorer, in the bafflement of things never-before-heard,
in that threatened clarity and nightingale river of the campsite,
from the miracle-working treasure itself, torrential, unnoticed,
flowing towards phases and reefs of temperature and methods unknown.

*

Los valses nupciales en mazurca de tentáculos prodigiosos,
cristalinos, cabalgan los cerros en construcción de olivos
y acacias de disolución, corroyéndose a la borda llorante de colonos.
Los pinos-parciales, marciales en letargo, ostentan sus "rincones" fotográficos
en la pollera almidonada del turista.
En acordes de acordeón, con hielo brutal, narrativo,
cubriendo los planos de ensayo de apariencia y románticas,
los medallones plácidos, castellanos, pálidos de víspera con herrumbre
dan a Bogotá, la erótica, místicas mantillas de beatitud.
Al fondo dudable, embadurnado, incorpóreo, el declinado lila de la adolescencia mañanera,
y la esquila amartillada del gitano sin cabaña de nogal y retamo.
El labrador impávido escarbando el destino de su silla de mimbre
sin explicarse las telarañas del semblante y su pipa funeral.

*

The wedding-day mazurka waltzes, with enormous grasping reach,
transparent, ride over the hills to go build dissolving olive trees
and acacias, eroding at the weeping huts of tenant farmers.
The partial-pines, lethargic militiamen, flaunt their photographic "corners"
in the starched skirt of the tourist.
Accordion chords, with brutal ice, narrative,
covering good-looking and romantic essay outlines,
and the tranquil medallions, Castilian, pale on the eve and rusting,
give to Bogotá the erotic, mystic mantillas of holiness.
At heart they are doubtful, greased, incorporeal, the declined lilac of early-rising adolescence
and the hammering cowbell of the gypsy with no shack of walnut and retamo trees.
The stone-faced farm worker poking at fate from his wicker chair
without explaining to himself the cobwebs on his face or his mournful pipe.

*

La arquitectura ciclópea (gasas-granjas, abrojos, juventud, forma y sombra),
lanchas —ademán y mineral— que zarpan conciliando polillas y alacranes.
Si allí es paréntesis tempestuoso y combustible confidencial,
aquí es trizadura de carreteras, arbustos o vertientes de la armadura sensata.
Las cordilleras esponjan sus caderas de azogue
en un desplazamiento de rastrojos acres que ralean.
Allá el clavel del aire y los proverbios misioneros-presurosos del viviente
con su imán de correrías y atrapando en el dintel de los miosotis
el tamiz de un cuadro momentáneo con retrato, vaina y corte metropolitano.
"La bella sultana del valle:" Cali y la calva genial de Jorge Isaacs
todo blanco, todo María,[5] todo blanco el ave negra de coral.
Montaña-línea de cuaderno, listado, escolar, estampillas,
miriñaque sensorial, la égloga inanimada, invocación, folleto,
alentando en la pátina de lo cierto y su cilicio patente.

---

[5] Se refiere al personaje cuyo nombre da título al libro del escritor y poeta romántico colombiano Jorge Isaacs (1837–1895), *María*, publicada en 1867.

*

The gigantic architecture (crêpe-farms, thistles, youth, form and shadow),
boats – gesture and mineral – that set sail reconciling moths and scorpions.
If there is stormy parentheses and confidential fuel,
here is crack-up of roads, bushes or hills with prudent armour.
The cordilleras swagger their quicksilver hips
in a shifting of stubble acres, growing sparse.
There is air carnation[14] and missionary-hasty proverbs of the living,
with their magnet for escapades, trapping on the lintel of forget-me-nots,
a sieve, the fleeting image, portrait of scabbard and urban court.
"The beautiful sultana of the valley": Cali and the great bald head of Jorge Isaacs,
all white, all María,[15] all white the black bird of coral.
Mountain-line from notebook, inventory, schoolkid, stamps,
sensory hoop skirt, lifeless eclogue, invocation, pamphlet,
encouraging in its patina of certainty and its obvious hair shirt.

---

[14] *clavel del aire*: A plant, literally air carnation, found in Colombia (as well as Chile). It has this name due to its light seeds and silky parachutes, which give it a tendency to float and cling to surfaces.
[15] María is the eponymous protagonist of the romantic Colombian novel *María* by Jorge Isaacs (1837–1895). She wears a *clavel del aire* in her hat, which wilts before the return of her lover.

*

Por el hechizo pudoroso de cisterna verde-azul o cuervos, estiércol,
cascabeles en hilera hacia la negrura plural de los milenios, (barcarolas tristes).
En total esplendidez de amor romero, en clarividencia morena,
adornada del brinco bravío de los grillos fecundos y sonámbulos.
Dibujo-plegado de un eslabón perdido y contraído, corvo herido,
con clavo de diamante rodando, sin letras, viñeta, alhucema,
consagrando un juego con el lechoso argumento veterano, erupción
de un almanaque sin cálculo mortal en tres pilares individuales
y una pre-historia en bajorrelieve, gemela y espeluznante.
Desmigajo el bloque horizontal, ladino, de incertidumbre
de las mensajeras en vértigo, centinelas de la fugacidad y el péndulo,
emisor-atómicas de una hora jovial, de un día en gestación,
de un siglo por postdata, de una eternidad y un insecto.

*

Through the modest spell of green-blue cistern or ravens, dung,
little bells in a row towards the plural blackness of millennia (sad barcarolles).
In total splendour of pilgrim love, in dark-featured clairvoyance,
adorned with the savage jump of fertile sleepwalking crickets.
Folded sketch of a lost contracted link, wounded hook,
with diamond spike rolling, without letters, vignette, lavender,
blessing a game with milky veteran plot, eruption
of an almanac without mortal calculation in three individual pillars
and a prehistory in bas-relief, twinned and spine-tingling.
I crumble the horizontal block, ladino, uncertain
as dizzy messengers, sentinels of fleetingness and pendulum,
atomic-transmitters of a cheerful hour, of a gestating day,
of a century by postscript, of an eternity and an insect.

*

Arrullo, sin querer, en mi regazo, un agudo silencio devorador
en torno a la cadencia que suministran los míos lienzos viajeros sobre una superficie de cristal.
He aquí, Pablo de Rokha, el monólogo enroscado al desolado cáliz-delirante
de la incomprensible, amarga y misteriosa infancia de América y sus cangrejos dorados.
Desdoblado por cobalto de amaneceres sin rumbo y céfiros,
o rústico calado de oro y plata por himno y por cabeza contemporánea,
granítico añil local que evoca delirios, noticia, análisis, leyenda,
de lo quedado atrás: plumaje, ladrillo, y soledad inevitable.
Emoción de metal entre metales del Titicaca-silabario
ídolo de doble y triple dentadura planetaria, panteísta, banderola, contumaz,
abyecta de mirlos como trompos subjetivos.
Ni rama, ni pez, ni brizna, ni sien de olvido, herida.
Amalgama de caracoles adheridos a la perspectiva infinita,
ajadas serranías, cavernas, abruptos peñascales, rebelión, melancolía
y lechuzas sentadas, piojos, miasmas, monos y enormes vientos.

*

I sing a lullaby, without willing it, to the intense all-consuming silence in my lap,
turning about the rhythm supplied by my paintings travelling over a glass surface.
Here, Pablo de Rokha, is my convoluted monologue to the forlorn delirious-chalice
of the incomprehensible, bitter, mysterious childhood of América and its golden crabs.
Unfurled by the cobalt of dawns without destination and by zephyrs,
or by rustic fretwork of gold and silver, by hymn and by contemporary head,
this local granite indigo evokes deliriums, news, analysis, legend,
about what was left behind: plumage, brick and inevitable solitude.
Emotion of metal amongst metals from the Titicaca-syllabary,
idol with double and triple dentures, planetary and pantheist, a banderole, stubborn,
wretched as blackbirds subjective as whirling tops.
Neither branch, nor fish, nor blade of grass, nor temporal bone of oblivion, nor wound.
Amalgam of snails that cling to infinite perspective,
aged mountain ranges, caverns, steep crags, rebellion, melancholy
and perched owls, lice, vapours, monkeys and fierce winds.

www.ingramcontent.com/pod-product-compliance
Lightning Source LLC
Chambersburg PA
CBHW080551170426
43195CB00016B/2758